LAST RITES

THE

FINAL DAYS

OF THE

BOSTON

MOB WARS

WILLIAM J. CRAIG

Charleston  London

THE
History
PRESS

Published by The History Press
Charleston, SC 29403
www.historypress.net

First published 2009

All images are by the author unless otherwise noted.

Manufactured in the United States

ISBN 978.1.59629.834.7

Library of Congress Cataloging-in-Publication Data

Craig, William J., 1972-
Last rites : the final days of the Boston mob wars / William J. Craig.
p. cm.
Includes bibliographical references.
ISBN 978-1-59629-834-7
1. Mafia--Massachusetts--Boston--Case studies. 2. Marino, Vincent, 1960- 3.
Gangsters--Massachusetts--Boston--Case studies. 4. Organized crime--Massachusetts--
Boston--Case studies. I. Title.
HV6452.M42M343 2009
364.1'0609744--dc22
2009040849

This book is dedicated to my precious wife Charlene. She has been the backbone of my life. She has given me strength when I had none and continued love and support throughout my ventures, no matter what path I chose. If I ever needed a reason to become a better person she gave me the reason, and our daughter Meadow Jean has given me the chance. I love you both and I promise my love will never falter.

Contents

Author's Note

This is a work of nonfiction. Most of the spoken words were taken from interviews, wire taps, court testimonies and newspaper articles, were reconstructed by eyewitnesses to the events or have been recounted to me. I have attributed thoughts to some of the characters, and all of these were plausibly described to me. I describe criminal proceedings and cite various documents relating to them.

While growing up in Revere, I have not only personally known the men mentioned in this book, such as Sean Cote, Paul Strazzula, Eddie Portalla and Gigi Portalla, but I have associated with them from time to time as well. I have had and continue to have a very close personal friendship with the Portalla family. I also personally know and have interviewed some of the Revere Police officers mentioned in this book. Many of the stories and their details have never been revealed until now.

Acknowledgements

I would like to take this opportunity to thank my father-in-law, Mike Devaney, for all his time and effort in reviewing this manuscript prior to publication. To my stepchildren, Cory Devaney, Kyle Ferguson and Leah Ferguson, thank you for your patience and understanding while my time was taken up with research and writing. I would also like to extend my heartfelt appreciation and gratitude to Grandma Dorothy Devaney for all her care packages that she mailed from Kansas City, Missouri, to the family while this project was being undertaken. I can't forget my favorite bartender, Scott Devaney, whose prompt service is always appreciated. At this time, I would also like to thank Ray Regan for his constant friendship and advice and M.G. for his friendship and caring, especially toward my family and daughter. Grateful appreciation should also be extended to my brother, author James Craig, for his assistance in finding The History Press and guiding me in their direction for the publication of this book. Last but not least, special thanks need to be extended to my dear friend Ed Portalla for his assistance, friendship and advice throughout the years.

Introduction

The nefarious, blood-stained culture of the Italian-American underworld has long been a spectacle of attraction for the American public. These men have been romanticized, mystified into men of honor and propelled into American idol status. In reality, they are sociopathic deviants who traverse a depraved world. Their charisma is dark, and their chilling presence bodes ill tidings to the law-abiding public. These men and their world tap into a part of us that we manage to keep hidden even from ourselves. This is true because organized crime exists to serve our primal human appetites. The appetite could be drugs, the urge to make a fast buck or to get laid by someone other than your wife.

The main tool of the mafia trade is intimidation, and undeniably, intimidation works. Just think how quickly we would pay our bills if the threat of bodily harm were thrown into the mix instead of a late payment notice. The inevitable carnage that comes with mob life is only a byproduct of doing business. First and foremost, organized crime is a business. The main objective of any entrepreneurial endeavor is to make money, or rather, to earn. The workload is constant and oftentimes exasperating. Much of the work revolves around bill collecting. The hours are sometimes long and brutal, and your co-workers are all thieves. However, there is an upside. There are no pension plans, health plans, audits or taxes to deal with. What you earn you keep, except for a small portion that is kicked up to the people above you as a form of tribute. For these men, crime is what they do, not who they are. There are no feelings

Gigi's graduation photo from Revere High School, 1980. *Courtesy of Revere High School.*

of guilt. This is a world where family lines, business lines and generational lines constantly cross and merge.

For many years, organized crime in Massachusetts has been viewed as a weak and pesky stepchild when compared to organized crime in New York or Chicago. However, once the underhanded dealings between Whitey Bulger, a South Boston gang boss, and the FBI were broadcast across the national news networks and *America's Most Wanted*, this opinion quickly changed. The American public quickly became aware of just how prevalent organized crime was in New England and in the Boston district of the FBI.

This is the story of Gigi Portalla, aka Vincent Marino, a man well known within the New England organized crime cabal as well as law enforcement circles. Gigi is a unique and surprising man. He stands six feet, three inches, and weighs in at 250 pounds of pure muscle. He is intimidating to look at; however, he is extremely well spoken and courteous. His life does not follow the stereotypical mobster story. Rather, this book follows a young man's personal journey for direction and understanding in a world few rarely see. He is also probably the last standup guy of the mafia generation. Unlike other racketeers, he did not sell out every one of his crime associates to stay out of prison. Instead, he is serving a thirty-five-year sentence in federal prison. Leading up to Gigi's incarceration, an attempt was made on his life. He was severely wounded during a botched mob hit, and controversy surrounded certain circumstances in the aftermath of that incident. While he was undergoing surgery for his wound, it is widely believed that the FBI and DEA planted a tracking device in his buttocks. Both bureaus have denied this accusation, all the while not allowing Mr. Portalla to undergo the necessary medical tests to prove his case. The denials come from the same FBI field office that is responsible for the Whitey Bulger fiasco, raising some serious doubts on the credibility of their stated denials. Gigi's life mirrors the life of a true, tragic Machiavellian hero.

This book is more than a rare look into a repulsive criminal world that not only celebrates, but rewards, the self-destructive behavior of people who are devoid of conscience and bereft of human decency or morality. It is a story of personal reflection and how the choices we make today will dictate the life we lead tomorrow.

CHAPTER 1

THE BOTCHED HIT

In the early morning hours of Sunday, November 24, 1996, a nondescript Chrysler parked on a North Shore road outside of a local watering hole called Club Caravan in Revere, Massachusetts. Although it was a chilly fall night, the club was still a flurry of activity. A few local patrons braved the wind coming off the ocean as they hurried into the bar to make last call. The driver of the Chrysler exited the vehicle and approached a solitary man waiting on the sidewalk in front of the club. The two men began arguing, with the shorter man explaining that he needed more time to raise the money. At the same time, a black Lincoln Continental pulled up across the street from the Chrysler. Suddenly, a Bronco screeched up to the club. The driver slipped on a pair of gloves, exited the vehicle high on cocaine and headed toward the two men arguing. Instinctively, the taller man turned toward the man approaching from the Bronco and began to wrestle over a gun that had its barrel oiled in case of this scenario. The peaceful night quickly erupted with the sound of gunfire and shattering glass, as the man in the Lincoln began to shoot at the passenger in the Chrysler. The driver of the Chrysler scrambled into the nightclub, pushing past patrons and security in an attempt to evade his would-be assassins, and lurched toward the band only to collapse on the dance floor from a wound in his buttocks. The passenger of the Chrysler managed to crawl into the driver's seat amidst the flying bullets and shattering glass, only to drive the car approximately fifty yards down the road, where he ran into the Wonderland Ballroom before collapsing from his wounds.

The Caravan Club, looking the same as it did the night Gigi was shot.

Almost immediately, Revere Police, on a traffic detail at nearby Wonderland Dog Track, responded to both scenes. Both men were well known to the police. The driver who was wounded in the buttocks was Vincent Marino, aka Gigi Portalla, a thirty-five-year-old Revere native. The other man was twenty-nine-year-old Charles McConnell, aka Fat Charlie. Club Caravan had about 150 people inside who were uninjured even though a bullet passed through two panes of glass and ricocheted inside the club. The sidewalk outside of the club was littered with shell casings and glass. Gigi was placed on a service table and EMTs began working on him. The police, fearing that McConnell would die from his wounds before an ambulance could arrive, asked him who the attempted assassins were. McConnell answered in true Cagney style, "I'm no rat," while lying in a pool of his own blood.

As both men were being transported to Massachusetts General Hospital, a Toyota Camry came racing up to Club Caravan. As Revere Police detectives approached the car, they realized that it was Gigi's brother, Eddie Portalla. Eddie had received a call from his mother, who was frantic due to her son just being shot. So he left his home to find out what was happening to alleviate her fears. As he spoke with detectives and looked over the Chrysler riddled with bullets and shattered glass, a call came in over the police radio about another shooting. This one had taken place in the parking lot of the Comfort Inn located on the Revere–Saugus line. Only this time, the gunmen didn't miss.

The Final Days of the Boston Mob Wars

Revere Police detectives and Eddie drove to the scene only to find the lifeless, bullet-ridden body of Robert Nogueira lying covered in the parking lot with his middle finger sticking straight up, under a sign promising a free continental breakfast. According to witnesses, as Nogueira lay bleeding on the pavement just feet away from the guest room windows, the killer pumped two more slugs into his head. Hotel guest Loretta Westcott, who heard the mob hit, stated, "I'll never stay in Revere again." Nogueira had been struck by at least ten bullets at approximately 1:30 a.m. He had been living at the Comfort Inn under an assumed name and was a friend of Gigi Portalla and Robert McConnell. Nogueira was from Charlestown, Massachusetts, and had served twelve years for bank robbery at the Braintree branch of the Hancock Bank and Trust Company. His criminal career was begun at age eighteen, when he was arrested for a Melrose Bank heist.

After being questioned by detectives, Eddie proceeded to Massachusetts General Hospital to console his mother and check on his brother's condition. When he arrived at the hospital, he found Charlie McConnell under police guard and in stable condition. McConnell had been hit in the back and arm. Gigi was operated on, but the doctors operated again, claiming that an infection had set in. All the while, he was isolated from his family. Once the Portalla family was assured that he was going to live, they went home for the night.

Meanwhile, the police were just beginning their investigation. At 4:00 a.m., the police recovered a black Lincoln Continental that had been torched nearby on the Winthrop–East Boston line. The car had been reported stolen a few hours earlier from a Boston livery company and matched the description of the gunmen's vehicle that had been seen speeding away from Club Caravan after the shooting. The Revere Police had conducted interviews with the 150 patrons inside Club Caravan as well as the customers of the Wonderland Ballroom. One of the suspects had left his mother's car at the shooting scene, and in the trunk a bulletproof vest and ammo were discovered. In the days that followed, the police continued to gather information from informants, State Police and the Federal Bureau of Investigations.

They soon realized that a shooting that had occurred earlier in October 1996 was tied to the events that had recently taken place at Club Caravan on that cold November night. A local paralegal named Frank Imprescia, who was fifty-seven years of age, had been shot and wounded in October. Frank had been sitting at his desk in the law office of Attorney Leonard

Pass, located on busy Revere Beach Parkway. An unknown gunman had fired three rounds through the front window of the office, striking Frank and seriously wounding him in the torso. The investigation at the time revealed that the gunman had parked at the Esquire Club and walked through a trailer park, allowing him to approach the law office from behind almost undetected. Luckily, at the time the shots were fired, Attorney Pass had been in the bathroom. Imprescia had recently been released after serving a three-and-a-half-year prison term for extortion and had been linked to reputed mob boss Joseph Russo and former high-ranking Boston mobster Ralph Lamattina. Joseph "J.R." Russo is best known for fulfilling the contract that was put out on Joe "the Animal" Barboza on February 11, 1976, in San Francisco.

With all this information tallied, Revere Police came to the realization that their worst fears were coming true and that a full-scale mob war had begun. A power struggle was taking place for control of the New England turf. On one side was the Portalla crew, the non-Salemme faction, and on the other side were Frank "Cadillac Frank" Salemme and his followers. As Gigi lay in the hospital bed recovering from his wound, he began to reflect back on his life. At some point, a choice is made and fate is established. People arrive at a crossroads, and the path they choose determines the rest of their journey. Some call it destiny or providence. Others call it chance. Gigi thought back on where his crossroads had been and in what direction he was heading.

CHAPTER 2

GROWING UP IN REVERE

The city of Revere is located approximately five miles north of downtown Boston. It is perhaps best known for its three-mile uninterrupted view of the Atlantic Ocean, which was America's first public beach. During the late nineteenth and early twentieth centuries, the area was billed as the Playground of New England. Amusement entrepreneurs built a thoroughfare of rides, ballrooms and elegant nightclubs. Many big-name stars played here, including Tommy Dorsey, Jerry Vale, Louis Prima and Barbra Streisand. In 1923, the Massachusetts Senate voted to allow gambling. Revere then became home to Suffolk Downs Racetrack and Wonderland Dog Track. Suffolk Downs has the distinction of being the track from whence Triple Crown Winner Seabiscuit was claimed.

Revere is also home to many hardworking immigrant families who are in search of a better life. In the era when Gigi grew up, Revere was segregated by ethnic enclaves of Italians, Irish and Eastern European Jews. Each enclave was a tightly knit community that proudly displayed its own ethnic culture. The Jewish section of the city centered on Shirley Avenue. The Ave, as it is still affectionately called, had a pool hall, delicatessens and bakeries that catered to the needs of its neighbors. In later years, after the mass exodus of Jewish residents to the suburbs, the slow decline of the area began. The Beachmont section was predominantly Irish and had its own eccentricities that made it stand out from the rest of the city. The majority of the city was Italian, and every October, no matter what your ethnic background, everyone celebrated Christopher Columbus Day. After the parade, the

The Frolic Nightclub, which was the mob's hangout on Revere Beach.

smell of barbecued sausage and peppers hung in the air thicker than a fog in London. Large crowds gathered in and around the many Italian social clubs around the city to converse about the parade and the food. Revere kids mostly came from hardworking blue-collar families. These families are what the politicians refer to as the "working poor." They have a roof over their heads, food on the table, a ten-year-old car and a house full of used furniture. As for the extras, like new clothes or money for an ice cream, these are few and far between.

Most of the neighborhoods near the beach look poor and uninviting. Many of the bars are dark, dingy and shadowy places. They reek of thousands of days and nights of heavy smoking and boozing. The windows are tinted yellow with nicotine, and the dark wood paneling is greasy and filthy. It is in these dark places that the boils on the ass of society congregate to prey on the weak and needy.

With poverty being a common thread among the kids of Revere, defense of one's own property is a must. Kids learn early on that theft is a means of acquiring the extras in life. This means that they must be ready to fight anyone to keep the little bit they do have. Otherwise, they end up with nothing very fast. Kids in Revere grow up fast and are not under any delusions about the harsh realities of life. A kid must learn to fight at an early age, not only

The Final Days of the Boston Mob Wars

Mr. Buccola, the boss of the New England mafia prior to Raymond Patriarca. *AP worldwide.*

to protect what he has but also to prove that he has heart. It doesn't matter whether he wins or loses, as long as he stands up for himself. Mental and physical toughness are the keys to survival. Toughness establishes respect—respect of self and respect from one's peers. Once respect is established, the bonds of friendship are made, which will last a lifetime.

Revere youth inevitably receive two distinct educations from within the city perimeter. The first education comes from their parents, church and local school. They learn about family, God, reading, writing, mathematics and government. The other education comes from their neighborhood and their surroundings. They quickly realize that the city has two police departments. The first is uniformed and run by city hall, like every community police department in the country. The second group of enforcers is much less conspicuous but ever present. They drive Cadillacs, dress in expensive suits and wield unlimited power. They control every aspect of life in the city, although covertly. The youth of Revere watch them in awe as they interact outside of barrooms and social clubs. They mimic their manners of speech and hand gestures.

Revere is a place where the past is more alive and more defining than the future—a city where local racketeers are not only protected by their neighbors but also celebrated for their actions. Gigi came of age in this world.

The New England mafia can trace its heritage back to the year 1916, when Gaspare Messina started the family in Boston. Messina was succeeded by Phil Buccola when he passed away in 1924. Under Buccola, the family enlarged certain staple enterprises such as loan sharking, numbers and bootlegging. Buccola's reign was low key until 1950, when the Kefauver hearings began. Fearing public exposure for his illicit activities, Buccola had

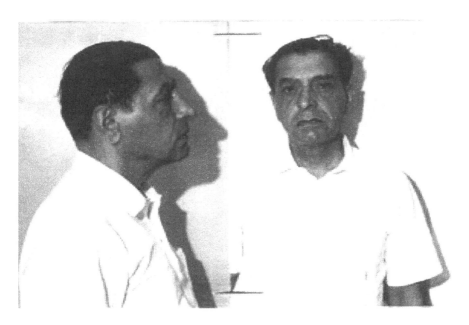

Raymond Patriarca Sr., ruler of the New England mafia for several decades. *AP worldwide.*

Joseph Lombardo, who was in charge of gaming, shut down all bookmaking operations. This order opened the door for bookmakers to operate more freely, although they didn't have mob protection.

Raymond Patriarca was born to Italian immigrants in Worcester, Massachusetts, in 1908. When Patriarca was four years old, his parents moved to Providence, Rhode Island. He left school at the age of eight to shine shoes and work as a bellhop at a local hotel. Eventually, Patriarca discovered that armed robbery and smuggling liquor during Prohibition paid better than lugging suitcases. During the 1930s, the Providence Board of Public Safety branded him "Public Enemy No. 1" and ordered the police to arrest him on sight. In 1938, Patriarca went to jail for armed robbery. He was sentenced to five years but only served a few months. The reduced sentence caused legislators in Massachusetts to inquire into the pardon that he had received. The pardon was granted by then Governor Charles F. Hurley Jr. It turned out that a prime factor behind the pardon was a heart-rending plea from a fictitious Catholic priest named Father Fagin. It came out later that the governor's right-hand man, Executive Councilor Daniel Coakley, had drawn up the pardon and passed it through the proper officials in order to have it granted. Coakley was later impeached and barred from ever holding another public office in the state. The scandal only helped to solidify Patriarca's standing as a man with political connections. By the early 1940s, Patriarca had assumed a major leadership role within the mafia.

Of interest, an essential operation at this time was Pinetree Stables in Framingham, Massachusetts. The rambling acres, expensive barns and lushly appointed main house served a hidden purpose. Outwardly, it was a breeding farm for thoroughbred racing horses. Its real purpose, however, was as a secluded, heavily guarded sanctuary for national mob meetings. Plush limousines would arrive every Sunday at the main house to meet with Massachusetts crime boss Joseph Lombardo. Some of the farm's noteworthy visitors included Carlos Marcella of Louisiana, known as the "little man," and Anthony "Fat Tony" Salerno from New York, a representative of Charles "Lucky" Luciano. These are the men who would eventually turn the New England territory over to Patriarca in the years to come.

In the 1950s, Patriarca assumed command of the New England mob. For a quarter of a century, he built his power base with little public exposure and law enforcement scrutiny. During the early 1950s, Las Vegas was just beginning to become the adult Disneyland, and the casino boom was almost completely financed with mob money. Ben "Bugsy" Siegel built the Flamingo hotel and casino; the Thunderbird was financed by Meyer Lansky, although he had small pieces of other casinos as well; the Desert Inn was owned by Moe Dalitz and the Cleveland mob; the Sands was owned by Frank Costello, Joe Adonis and actor George Raft; the Sahara and Riviera were owned by Tony Arcado, Sam Giancana, Nicholas Civella (boss of the Kansas City mob) and Frank Costello; and the Dunes was owned by Frank Costello and Raymond Patriarca. When Caesar's Palace was being built, the top investors were Tony Arcado, Patriarca, Jerry Catena (a top aide of Vito Genovese) and Vicent Alo, a longtime friend of Meyer Lansky. As the mob bosses perfected the practice of skimming millions of dollars from the Las Vegas casinos, investors such as Raymond Patriarca were able to fill their coffers and use skim money to increase their power base over their respective territories. Patriarca's Las Vegas investments made him an extremely wealthy and powerful man.

The head of the Massachusetts State Police once told a legislative committee that Patriarca was so ruthless and devious that he regularly hijacked liquor shipments that he was hired to protect. The ruthlessness of Patriarca extended all the way to his own men. Once Patriarca put up $20,000 for his men to handle a load of stolen cigarettes. The FBI had other plans and seized the load. Patriarca was uninterested in why the shipment had been lost. His sole interest was in getting his money back. The men had to scrounge around and come up with the $20,000 in order to pacify their boss. Patriarca was always a partner in the profits but never in losses. Patriarca was once heard ordering a hit on his own brother on an FBI wiretap. Evidently, his brother had failed to find a bug in his office while he was in charge of mob security. Patriarca eventually called off the hit and welcomed his brother back into the fold.

Then Joseph Barboza, a Patriarca enforcer and hit man turned informer, brought forth a devastating blow to the Patriarca family. Law enforcement was able to convict Patriarca of conspiracy to commit murder, specifically having made man Rocco DiSiglio killed for being a fingerman for a stickup gang that was robbing mob crap games. While serving the six-year prison sentence, Patriarca was able to run his mob from behind bars, much like Vito Genovese, thereby opening the door for freelance racketeers such as Jerry Angiulo to move in and shake down bookies. In 1954, Buccola fled to Sicily and left the family in the care of Raimondo Laredo Salvatore Patriarca. Once the New York Commission approved of Patriarca, he would become the new boss and Buccola would be retired. Patriarca even lent out his top hit man, John "Jackie" Nazarian, to kill Albert Anastasia, aka the Mad Hatter, of Murder Inc. fame.

At 10:10 a.m. on October 25, 1957, two men on Seventh Avenue were obscured by the crowds passing by as they stepped from a sedan and headed into Manhattan's Park Sheraton Hotel. As the men entered the hotel behind a workman, they all walked briskly toward the barbershop of the hotel. The workman paused briefly at the barbershop, pointed a newspaper at the chair where Anastasia was sitting and then disappeared into the hotel. The two men then pulled up handkerchiefs that were tied around their necks and hid their faces. At 10:20 a.m., the barbershop erupted in gunfire. The hit was orchestrated by Tony Strollo, underboss of the Genovese family. He contacted Patriarca because most of the hit men in New York were terrified of Anastasia. The New York families wanted someone who wasn't scared and could complete the job without being detected by Anastasia. Needless to say, Nazarian was successful.

The Final Days of the Boston Mob Wars

Raymond Patriarca's headquarters on Atwell Avenue in Providence, Rhode Island. *AP worldwide.*

Patriarca moved the family headquarters from Boston to Providence shortly after taking power. His office on Atwell Street in Providence was an armed camp. This nondescript two-story building was, at least in theory, home to the National Cigarette Service Company and Coin o Matic Distributors. This setup was comparable to other mob strongholds such as Mulberry Street in New York's Little Italy and Prince Street in Boston. If you entered the Atwell Street office, you were greeted by at least two men at the door. They would escort you through a maze of cigarette and pinball machines, and past a repair area to an overhead steel door in the back. Once it was lifted up, you would enter a twelve- by twelve-foot room that served as the nerve center for the New England mob. It was from here that Patriarca ruled like a king on his throne.

From his office, he oversaw gambling, extortion, loan sharking, prostitution and truck hijackings. In the afternoon, he could be seen sitting out front in his beach chair, smoking a cigarette and greeting people as they walked by. Not only did every store owner on Atwell Avenue pay him protection money, but he also collected tribute from every bookie from Maine to New York.

This was the powerful and sinister leader—Raymond Patriarca—who, along with his organization, would become at least partially responsible for the future of Gigi Portalla.

CHAPTER 3

THE BOSTON UNDERWORLD

Gennaro "Jerry" Angiulo was born in 1919, the son of Sicilian immigrants who operated a small grocery store in the North End of Boston. During his early years, the North End was an overcrowded ghetto that was teeming with Italian and Sicilian immigrants who were all seeking a better life in the United States. The streets of the North End were narrow cobblestone and the tenement houses were small and congested, housing apothecaries, grocers and saloons. By the time the Angiulos were living in the North End, it was known to be Boston's most densely populated slum. The small waterfront neighborhood can trace its origins back to the earliest days of British settlement, prior to the Revolutionary War. As the original occupants of the North End grew in prosperity, they moved out of the North End. Most of the Protestant families fled to Beacon Hill, and Irish immigrants began moving into the neighborhood. Against the clamor of the teeming life in the streets was the stench of rotting food and wastes that were intermittently carted away by a neglectful sanitation department. Money lending and furniture stores were occupying what once had been prime commercial property. For a while, both Irish and Italian immigrants began to settle in the North End, but eventually the Irish moved out, creating their own enclave in the South End of Boston.

In some neighborhoods, the numbers game or policy flourished. Since the late 1800s, it had been particularly successful among the black neighborhoods. It was an illegal lottery run by small racketeers and, later, by crime syndicates. In the early days, bettors purchased a number, hoping that

Gennaro Angiulo, the numbers man of Boston. *AP worldwide.*

it would match a winning number to be drawn later in the day, usually from a bowl in an attic or garage. The disadvantage to this system was that it was easily rigged. To convince bettors that the game was on the level, it was linked to published horse-racing results at Suffolk Downs. This was called the handle, and it was very successful in the New England area. Newly arriving immigrants religiously played the numbers in an attempt to get rich quick in their new home.

During the 1920s, there weren't many opportunities for the newly arriving Italian immigrants. Although the Angiulo family had it a little better than most families living in the overcrowded squalor that was the North End, Jerry was looking for an easier way to earn a living. He was raised with five brothers and sisters on Prince Street, where he later set up his underworld headquarters. As a young man, he worked with his siblings in the small grocery store that their parents ran. During World War II, Jerry joined the United States Navy and served in the Pacific Theater of Operations as a landing craft operator with the U.S. Marines. After the war, Jerry returned to the North End and worked as a low-level bookmaker. By the early 1950s, organized crime in Boston was floundering. Phil Buccola had ceased all bookmaking activities due to the Kefauver hearings; this left the door open for bookmakers to freelance their operations without mob protection.

Angiulo, seeing an opportunity to advance his position and increase the size of his bankroll, acted quickly. He would send his henchmen to a list of local bookies to intimidate them into paying Angiulo tribute. The henchmen would go to the bars where the bookies operated and take the betting slips. The next day, the men would return to the bookies after the Suffolk Downs parimutuel numbers had been published in the newspaper. The men would then inform the bookmakers that they had hit the parimutuel with them, and then produce the bookies' own slips as proof.

Boston bookies quickly paid tribute to Angiulo on a weekly basis, due to the fact that they no longer were under the umbrella of mob protection. By paying weekly tribute, the bookies were ensuring that they would not be intimidated by Angiulo's henchmen again. Knowing that once Patriarca took control of the New England mob his position of authority may be in jeopardy, Angiulo had to act quickly. He decided to ingratiate himself to Raymond Patriarca and his organization, since he did not have the muscle or manpower to go head to head against the New England crime organization. Angiulo took $50,000 down to Rhode Island and offered it to Patriarca as a gift. Patriarca was so touched by the gesture that he offered Angiulo a position within the organization. Angiulo now had the full force and blessing of the New England mob behind him. He was also one of the few members of the mob who became a made member without committing a murder. Angiulo knew that you didn't advance in this business by working on your own. Learning comes from the experience and teaching from those farther down the road than you are.

Angiulo was truly a numbers man. He had an uncanny ability to manipulate numbers, which made the New England mob the most profitable family in the mafia. The diminutive Angiulo stood at only five feet, seven inches, yet he was intimidating to deal with. He demanded respect but was not a typical gangster. He was a businessman and attempted to settle quarrels by making money rather than ordering murders. Violence was used by him as a last resort.

On Friday, September 16, 1960, the Boston Police Racket Squad brought two North End brothers into Boston Municipal Court and charged them with assault and battery. The two brothers were Donato Angiulo, thirty-seven years old, of Prince Street, and Frank Angiulo, thirty-nine years old, of Friend Street. The two men were the brothers of Jerry Angiulo. The police raiding party went to the Central Parlor Frame Company, where the Angiulos took bets on telephones, only to find out that someone had cut off the lines. They called a telephone lineman, who traced the lines to an apartment nearby. The raiding party then hastened to the Beacon Hill home of Municipal Court judge Elijah Adlow to get an emergency search warrant. When they arrived back at the apartment, Boston detective Arthur McNamara was bombarded by three telephones that were hurled at him by a man escaping from a window on Prince Street. McNamara gave pursuit and eventually caught Donato Angiulo. At the same time, another officer was punched in the face by Frank Angiulo as he was attempting to gain entrance into the building. Deputy Superintendent John Slattery described the crowd of residents outside the apartment as "extremely hostile." As the raiding party reached the doorway to the apartment building, they were greeted by a snarling German shepherd dog. The dog's master was finally persuaded by the police to call the dog off. Meanwhile, someone in the crowd pulled two fire alarms. This act caused the street to become congested with fire apparatus, stalled vehicles and approximately one thousand residents shouting profanity. The raiding party was finally able to break through several plywood-reinforced doors to reach the apartment. Once inside, they found an empty room with a stove, upon which there were burning slips of paper, causing the room to fill with smoke. They were able to confiscate some telephones, two long tables surrounded by chairs and two air conditioners. The police eventually brought forth complaints against the owner of the Central Parlor Frame Company, a Revere man.

The Plymouth Mail Robbery took place on August 14, 1962, on Route 3 in Plymouth, Massachusetts. The take from the heist was $1.5 million in cash. The robbers fenced the money to Jerry Angiulo for $0.60 on the dollar. Angiulo would bury the money somewhere for ten years or so until it cooled off and then spend it. This incident illustrates the power that Angiulo had throughout the New England area.

His crew was extremely efficient and disciplined, and its monthly profits were staggering. Angiulo's eventual demise came from his own greed and arrogance. FBI agents were tipped off on how to bug his headquarters by Whitey Bulger and Stephen Flemmi. The two informants gave the FBI the layout of the headquarters, and the agents began to plan the bugging of his office. Once the bugging was authorized by a judge, the agents went to work. They blocked off Prince Street with a car with its hood up, appearing to have broken down. The bugging team then entered the office in the very early morning hours. They had to do this twice, and both times the plan worked perfectly. They were able to get in and out undetected. The agents also planted several cars outside of the club. In the cars' grills they planted video cameras so that they could watch who entered and left the office. These cameras ran on ten freshly charged batteries, enough current to keep the cameras running for almost twenty-four hours. The autos were

The building in the foreground is where Angiulo ran his entire empire on Prince Street in the North End. This is the same headquarters that the FBI was able to bug and bring forth an ironclad case against the Boston mob.

switched each morning at about 3:00 a.m. The agents actually began their day at midnight at a garage in Woburn. They would charge the batteries and place them in the trunk or under a pile of junk in the back seat. When it came time to switch the cars, one agent would walk to the vehicle, get in and watch in the rearview mirror. Once the agent saw the replacement vehicle approach, the parked car would pull out and the replacement car would park in the same spot. The driver would then exit the vehicle and disappear into the North End. This system ensured that the FBI would always have an unobstructed view of Angiulo's headquarters. At one point, a member of the Angiulo crew walked up to one of the vehicles and peered into the windows and grill but never detected the camera. There were other problems as well, like when the tires were slashed or the neighborhood kids would sit on the fenders and the camera would bounce up and down. The preferred cars for the job were a 1974 Nova, a 1972 Impala and a 1965 Rambler.

The FBI's greatest dilemma came when it became caught in a deadly chess game over the fate of a grand jury witness. Walter LaFreniere's involvement with the Angiulos began innocently enough in late 1980, when he went to a "bartooth" dice game in the North End with his father-in-law. His father-in-law was Louis Venios, who was the owner of the Mousetrap. LaFreniere's troubles began when his luck turned cold at a dice table and he went to the house for credit. Venios spoke to Jason Angiulo, Jerry's son, and received a $2,000 loan right at the table. Within a few weeks, LaFreniere became a pawn between the FBI and Angiulo. Only eighteen days after the FBI had planted the bug in the headquarters, LaFreniere walked into Angiulo's headquarters at 98 Prince Street and discussed his overdue loan with Frank Angiulo. The conversation was listened to intently by the FBI. The former Strike Force attorney, Wendy Collins, who handled the grand jury, stated, "We just picked Walter, just some guy to subpoena. He was bringing money in. No big deal." In addition, "Jerry Angiulo became so obsessed with it. Once Jason got implicated, man, he was off the wall." Once Jerry got wind of the grand jury, he immediately returned from Fort Lauderdale. It seems that Jason had broken the most sacred of the rules: he did business with a stranger who could tell the tale. He was supposed to use a soldier as a buffer. A wiretap had picked up Jerry Angiulo saying to Jason, "Frank and I made you the boss [of the bartooth game]. Nevertheless, you were the only boss with insulation. Skinny, Johnny O. and Candy. How did you allow yourself to sit at a table with Louis Venios's son-in-law that he could ask you right at the table for the fucking $2,000?"

As Jerry Angiulo plotted his strategy to combat the grand jury, the agents listened to his plans and formulated counter measures. On March 19, 1981, Jerry Angiulo pulled Richie Gambale aside as he entered 98 Prince Street. As he, Gambale and Peter Limone huddled near the blaring television and cheap vinyl chairs in the front office, he turned the television even louder. It was 9:29 p.m., and the FBI agents were listening from the bug that they had installed right above where the three men were standing. Gambale was a thirty-nine-year-old enforcer who knew what the meeting was about. Jerry Angiulo was heard saying, "Sh, sh, sh, sh. Don't you ever raise your voice with me...You don't have to make the decisions. That's why I'm the boss."

The agents listening in were in an apartment in Charlestown. They received the signal from the bug through a scrambled radio signal. As the agents listened, it became more apparent that a future hit on LaFreniere was being discussed. The FBI high command had to be sure and then they needed to act quickly. If they notified LaFreniere of the hit, it would tip off Jerry Angiulo that a bug was in his office, and the next morning surveillance equipment would be thrown all over Prince Street. Angiulo reviewed his options on how to deal with LaFreniere. It seems that LaFreniere was into Gambale for money that he was collecting for Jerry Angiulo's brother Donato, who was the major loan shark in the North End. This meant that LaFreniere's testimony could possibly put Gambale away too. Jerry Angiulo ended the conversation by saying, "You ain't got a hot car. You ain't got nothin'. You think I need tough guys? I need intelligent tough guys. Well what do you want me to say? Do you want me to say to you—do it right or don't do it…Tell him to take a ride, okay?…You stomp him. Bing. You hit him in the fucking head and leave him right in the fucking spot. Meet him tonight…Just hit him in the fucking head and stab him, okay. The jeopardy is just a little too much for me. You understand American? Okay, let's go."

This conversation caused three agents to head directly over to the Mousetrap club in Park Square to inform LaFreniere and possibly flip him to the side of the government. About midnight, three agents walked through the door of the strip club. Agent Quinn, who had served LaFreniere with a summons ten days earlier, scoured the smoke-filled club looking for him. Quinn then left the club and called LaFreniere's wife at their Woburn home from the lobby of the Park Plaza Hotel. His wife lied and said that he wasn't home, so Quinn hung up the telephone and headed for Woburn. From a Purity Supreme parking lot near LaFreniere's home, they called him again, and this time he answered. He informed Quinn that he didn't want to talk. Quinn stated, "Fine. I don't want you to say anything to me. I just want you to listen. It's a matter of life and death, specifically yours. You don't have to believe me just hear me out." After Quinn informed him of what was about to go down, LaFreniere hung up the telephone and raced to the parking lot to meet with Quinn.

When he arrived at the lot at about 2:00 a.m., he exited his vehicle and clambered into the backseat of Quinn's car. After LaFreniere received the details of his possible execution, he informed the agents that he had been called by the Angiulos already and had a meeting set up with them in the morning. LaFreniere then promised to call Quinn the next morning, but he never did. Instead, he reached out to his father-in-law, who put him in touch with Danny Angiulo, who sent him to the family's attorney, William Cintolo. He informed LaFreniere not to talk and relayed all questions from the grand jury to Angiulo. Cintolo was later convicted of conspiring to obstruct justice.

By 4:00 p.m. on March 20, Angiulo had been briefed on Gambale's aborted attempt to meet up with LaFreniere and kill him. He reassessed the situation and decided to tell LaFreniere to shut his mouth and do eighteen months for contempt. In early April, Cintolo attempted to represent both Angiulo and LaFreniere. However, Strike Force attorney Wendy Collins argued successfully that it was a conflict of interest since LaFreniere was supposed to have been killed to save Jason Angiulo. Angiulo had a high regard for Venios, who had been paying the Angiulos juice for years. Every Saturday, Venios would get in his green Lincoln sedan and drive to the North End from his Combat Zone business. Although he was highly regarded as a standup guy, when he was behind on debts that carried 200 percent interest, he got no sympathy. When Venios was critically ill on oxygen in the hospital, Angiulo sent his brother Mike to go and inform him that it was in his best interest to be sure that he paid the money to Angiulo as soon as he left the hospital. Angiulo tried and tried to figure out how the government knew his every move, but he couldn't figure it out. He assumed that the FBI had bugged Gambale's car. He eventually found out through his network of eyes in the North End that the FBI was videotaping his office. He never had a clue about the wiretaps in his headquarters. Near the end, when the FBI was kicking in doors in the North End and grabbing evidence of gambling to go with the tape recordings, Angiulo would bring it all back to LaFreniere. Angiulo said, "Soon as that kid got a fucking summons, that was the beginning. We all fell asleep…It was like, it was like God sending us a fucking message, and we couldn't read it." He went on to say, "Why should I go to jail in this fucking thing, you know how many fucking things I did worse than this?"

Unwittingly, Angiulo gave the government what he was determined they would never have—evidence of his direct participation in criminal conspiracies. In many ways, the carefully considered decision to call in the enforcer Richie Gambale was a needless risk that cost Angiulo his empire. He would lose everything over a strip joint bartender who never posed any real danger to him. Nevertheless, decades of secrecy and stealth had led to a kind of paranoia that turned a mild threat into a fatal obsession.

The FBI eventually compiled enough evidence to bring charges forth. Prosecutor Diane Kottmyer compared Angiulo and his co-defendants to a highly sophisticated and structured Fortune 500 company. The audiotapes had Angiulo bragging about his illegitimate profits and his unlimited power to be able to bribe any official. During his trial, Angiulo mumbled under his breath, "Splice, splice," to his lawyer, while the prosecution was playing the wiretap tapes.

The Final Days of the Boston Mob Wars

Jerry Angiulo was being held in the outdated Charles Street Jail in Boston while on trial because he was perceived as a possible flight risk. The Charles Street Jail was an overcrowded, one-hundred-year-old dilapidated stone jail on the banks of the Charles River. The inmates were living among the most horrid and unsanitary conditions imaginable. Rats were known to come up through the toilets and bite inmates, windows were broken out for ventilation in the summer and the heat worked intermittently in the winter. The jail was a sort of funhouse for psychopaths and deviants. But Angiulo wasn't just any inmate, and his status afforded him certain luxuries, such as never having to wait in line to use the telephones, having food brought in so he didn't have to eat the usual slop and bribing the guards to get a better cell. Life in prison is different for wise guys than other people. While a guest of the "Graybar Motel," he bought all the inmates on his cell block television sets so they would be quiet while he was consulting with his lawyers on his case. Another time, he bailed out a section of the jail so he could have peace and quiet at night.

In the end, the jury convicted him on twelve crimes under the RICO (Racketeer Influenced and Corrupt Organizations) Act, including extortion, loan sharking, obstruction of justice and racketeering. When he was sentenced to forty-five years in Leavenworth and fined $120,000, he responded, "Thank you, your honor. Do you mind if I sit down?" As he was exiting the courtroom after unsuccessfully arguing for a reduction to his sentence so he wouldn't have to die in jail, he said, "We'll have to outlive them all." While in prison, he managed to keep his sense of humor intact. As he was going into the prison theatre one day, he commented, "What's this, *The Great Escape*?" The guards didn't find it funny, however. The comment landed him in solitary confinement for one day. It seems that a fellow inmate who worked in the clothing room with him had escaped a few days prior.

Angiulo was released from federal prison in 2007 after serving a total of twenty-one years. He left the Devens Federal Medical Center in the early morning hours under the cover of darkness with as little fanfare as possible. He quietly resided in Nahant with his second wife, Barbara. He had two sons, Jason and Jerry, and a daughter; his eldest daughter died of a brain aneurysm. He quietly faded into obscurity and passed away on August 29, 2009, from kidney failure. His passing was hardly covered by the media due to the attention paid to Massachusetts senator Ted Kennedy's funeral.

Reflecting back on Angiulo's turbulent years of crime illustrates that although he tried to resolve mob problems without taking lives, there were necessary exceptions to this rule to protect the stability of the business. One particularly violent example occurred on November 12, 1959, when a worker in the Everett dump discovered the body of North End criminal Joseph "Augie" Demarco with six bullets in his head. The Everett dump was located about a mile from the city of Revere. Demarco was last seen in an after-hours club in Boston called the Coliseum, which was owned by the mob. A grand jury was convened in Middlesex Superior Court in Cambridge. The grand jury called six witnesses: Jerry Angiulo; Larry Zannino; Phil Waggenheim, a contract killer; Henry Noyes, a mob soldier; Peter Jordan, mayor of Revere; and Phil Cresta. No indictments were handed down. However, the unofficial story was that Augie Demarco was robbing Angiulo bookies. Augie's death served as a warning to other would-be criminals that Angiulo bookmakers were off limits. The fact that Revere mayor Peter Jordan was called to testify helps establish that the mob was firmly entrenched within the city of Revere and had protection from its politicians.

The Ebb Tide Lounge on Revere Beach Boulevard was a lounge and nightclub that was popular with the residents of Revere. The club was often frequented by off-duty Revere Police officers who were seeking an enjoyable night out with their wives or girlfriends. Often, the club would have live entertainment and a free buffet for the club-goers. Officially, the club was owned by Richard Castucci. His wife held the liquor license on the club because of his criminal record for forgery and various other charges. In later years, Richard Castucci was a FBI informant. One evening, a young Turk by the name of Joseph Barboza gave Castucci and his uncle, Arthur Ventola, the owner of Arthur's Farm, a hard time. Castucci spoke to Henry Tameleo and asked for protection. Tameleo granted the request. Almost immediately, word hit the street that the club was protected by the mob. The club was in operation from the 1950s until the 1970s. During this period, the club was owned and frequented by members of the New England mob. In fact, they used to have card and dice games upstairs. One night, Fats Domino went upstairs and decided to try his luck after playing to a sold-out crowd. While upstairs, he lost the money he had made for the evening and sold the house his jewel-encrusted cuff links so he could keep playing.

Another little-known secret of the club took place every Thursday afternoon. A nondescript vehicle would pull up to the club and a man would exit the vehicle and enter the club. A short time later, the man would leave the club and drive away. Unbeknownst to law enforcement, the man would then head to Rhode Island to give Patriarca his weekly share of what had been collected from local bookmakers by Angiulo. The Ebb Tide served as a collection facility for the Angiulo operation. Angiulo now had a very powerful partner, Raymond Patriarca.

A field report written by an unidentified agent of the FBI, dated April 15, 1975, stated that Castucci had recently purchased the Squire strip club located in Revere and that the previous owner was paying Anthony Cataldo, aka Max Baer, $250 per week in protection. Castucci, who also owned the Ebb Tide, was already paying Bulger weekly protection. Therefore, Castucci refused to pay Baer and Baer recruited his nephew, Butchie Cataldo, a Massachusetts state representative, to spearhead a crusade to try to close down the Squire or at least get the topless and bottomless dancers banned. The mayor of Revere at the time was William Reinstein, whose motto was "Let Revere be Revere." At the time, Reinstein was indicted in a corruption scandal involving the city's new high school. He survived three mistrials. His field report raises an important question as to why Castucci was paying Bulger when originally he was paying protection to the mob. This bit of information should have tipped off the FBI that Bulger was starting to push the Italian mob out of its long-held territory. It may have also helped to give them some insight into the fact that the Patriarca-Angiulo reign was in jeopardy. On the other hand, it may have been that the Italian mob and the Winter Hill Gang were working together and splitting the take by the mid-1970s. Unfortunately, the FBI field reports don't give a clear and decisive answer either way.

Chapter 4

The Early Years

Sometime in 1955, a seventeen-year-old neighborhood kid with a propensity for violence began working for the Angiulo faction as a debt collector. His name was Edward "Big Eddie" Marino, and he stood at six feet, two inches, with a solid muscular frame, thick, curly, dark hair and movie star looks. Big Eddie was extremely well liked in the neighborhood; he was friendly, outgoing and always willing to help anyone in trouble. By 1960, at the age of twenty-two, he was married and living in an apartment on Everett Street in East Boston with an infant son, Edward, and his wife Corrine was expecting again. Big Eddie was steadily moving up within the Angiulo organization, proving himself to be loyal and trustworthy. In other words, he was a man among men. However, he was not yet a made man.

On the night of September 24, he found himself in the Famous Café, a bar in the South End of Boston. That night, he was drinking with a man when a fight broke out between the man and a woman. When the man began beating the woman unmercifully, Big Eddie stepped in and proceeded to give the man a taste of his own medicine. The fight was quickly over, and Philip Spataro—a thirty-five-year-old resident of Hanover Street in the North End of Boston who was a bartender and co-owner of the Famous Café—ordered the man to leave.

The fighting man walked back into the bar at close to closing time, completely unnoticed by the patrons, who had put the earlier altercation behind them. The man saw Big Eddie at the bar still sitting there, talking

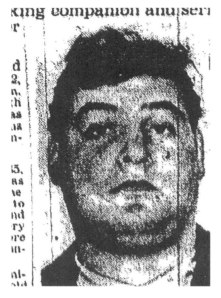

Left: *Boston American* photo of Ed Marino.

Below: The front page of the *Boston American* newspaper announcing Ed Marino's murder.

and laughing with his friends. He approached the bar and opened fire. Eddie collapsed to the floor, clenching his midsection, while the remaining twenty-five patrons ducked for cover. After the second shot, Spataro jumped over the bar and began to wrestle with the gunman, attempting to disarm him, when the gun discharged, hitting Spataro in the groin. The gunman then ran out of the bar on to Washington Street, where he fired another shot into the air before running up Dover Street. Boston Police Lieutenant John Donovan of the homicide squad said that police officers arrested a thirty-two-year-old South End man in a house on Middlesex Street. The gunman was in custody within two hours of the shooting. He was arrested by Sergeant George Bausch, Detective Thomas Carney, Patrick Hamilton and Edward Twohig. According to the police, the man was booked on suspicion of murder and assault and battery after being identified by Spataro at City Hospital. Spataro underwent surgery and eventually recovered from his wounds. Police thoroughly searched the premises on Middlesex Street, but the weapon was never found. Eddie died at the scene from two small caliber bullets lodged in his abdomen. The next day, U-2 pilot Francis Gary Powers was captured by the Soviets, Ted Williams announced his retirement, John F. Kennedy was preparing for his debate with Nixon and the *Boston American*'s front-page headline read "Man Slain in S.E. Bar." This one tragic event would have a devastating impact twenty years later.

Corrine Marino now found herself having to raise a child and bring another into the world without a father or husband to help her along the way. Within a few months, she gave birth to a healthy baby boy, whom she named Vincent. As time went on, Corrine met and eventually married a loving and hardworking man named Donald Portalla. Don was very accepting of Corrine's situation, and they both decided that it was in the best interest of the boys to have Don raise them as his own and keep the tragic incident of their father's murder from them. Don and Corrine went on to have three more children, two boys and a girl.

The family settled in Revere and lived in the housing projects off Broadway. The housing complex was a series of quaint duplexes with front and backyards. Don and Corrine both worked extremely hard to provide a stable, loving and nurturing home for the children. The children attended the Shurtleff School with other neighborhood children. Corrine raised her kids to be polite, courteous, studious and hardworking. Corrine and Don had taken every precaution to ensure that their children would stay on the right path of life. The neighborhood kids might be out on the corner until all hours, but their children had curfews. Eddie, the oldest, worked at Vazzas restaurant as a chef while maintaining an A average and graduating from Revere High School in 1979. The following year, Vincent, who was nicknamed Gigi, also graduated from Revere High School. Gigi had been a standout athlete in football and was voted king of the prom, elected to the student council and had aspirations of becoming

The Portalla homestead in the Revere projects. The apartment next to the one with the window boarded up is where the family lived for almost twenty years.

a Massachusetts State trooper. Since the age of thirteen, Gigi had worked in a local store slicing deli meats. Both boys had played instruments in the Saint Anthony's Church marching band. Eddie was accepted and enrolled in Bentley College and studied accounting. Gigi had enrolled at Bunker Hill Community College and began taking legal courses to help him pursue his dream of law enforcement. Don and Corrine Portalla had managed to help their children evade the pitfalls that so many young Revere kids can't help but trip on during their adolescent years.

Around this time, Corrine's father became gravely ill. As a last request before his passing, he asked her to promise that she would tell the boys the long-held family secret of their biological father. Reluctantly, she complied with his deathbed wish.

Once the family secret was revealed, it hit Gigi as strongly as when Paul was converted to Christianity by being stricken blind while on the road to Damascus. Gigi was now confronted with a dilemma: reject Eddie, his birth father, and his criminal behavior; or embrace his true father and inevitably become like him. Incapable of weighing the consequences of this greed gone mad, he had to make a choice that would shape who he was and who he would become. Eddie took the news a bit more in stride. Both boys wanted to know more about their hero father who had been cut down in his prime.

In 1981, Gigi went to the Angiulo headquarters in the North End of Boston on Prince Street. Jerry Angiulo was more approachable than most

Left: Eddie Portalla's yearbook photo from Revere High School, 1979. *Courtesy of Revere High School.*

Below: Vazza's Restaurant, where Eddie worked while in high school as a cook.

underworld figures. He was always willing to talk to the people of the neighborhood. This kind of goodwill helped to keep him insulated from law enforcement. Gigi approached him with the intention of working for him. Angiulo attempted to pacify him by saying that he was busy, but perhaps he could see him another time. Nevertheless, Gigi insisted, saying, "No, no you know my father. My father worked for you. He got killed, but I'm here and I wanna work for you guys, just like my father did." Still, it was to no avail; his pleas fell on deaf ears. But Gigi left determined to follow in his father's footsteps. During this same time, he took the Massachusetts State Police exam in hopes of possibly still becoming a trooper and making his mom proud and his dream a reality. He scored a ninety on the exam, which is truly impressive. Unfortunately, the state of Massachusetts had just implemented Proposition 2½, which severely limited spending statewide. This legislation

Gigi as a senior and captain of the football team. *Courtesy of Revere High School.*

Saint Anthony of Padua Church, where Gigi and Eddie attended Mass and played in the marching band.

meant that Gigi would not be hired since his test score was not high enough and he did not have veteran's status, which would raise him on the list of potential new troopers to be hired.

In 1983, he married his girlfriend, Gina Scarpa, and quickly settled into married life. His first arrest came in New Hampshire. He and three friends were parked in front of the Turkey Farm restaurant in Nashua. The Nashua Police noticed that one of the men fit the description of a man they were seeking in an armed robbery case. The officer initiated a traffic stop on the vehicle and proceeded to search the auto and its occupants. The search turned up guns and masks but nothing to link the men to an armed robbery. Gigi took a plea bargain offer and was sentenced to twenty-five months in a New Hampshire state prison on a simple gun charge. The district attorney and the police attempted to offer Gigi a guaranteed position in the Massachusetts State Police force if he would cooperate and help link his friends to the armed robbery. He declined their offer immediately, knowing that age-old adage that a rat is the worst thing anyone could ever be, especially for someone from Revere.

Gigi was introduced to organized crime almost by convenience. In Revere, wise guys are considered legitimate members of society. The citizens look out for them and protect them just as they would any member of their family. These mobsters had become an integral part of the social fabric, which helped make the city a unique place. These men of honor also bestowed certain benefits on the community, which made muggings, rapes and house break-ins almost nonexistent.

Revere was originally run by a Jewish gangster named Lou Fox from 1947 until 1962. He was of medium height, well dressed and always very polite and respectable. Fox had an office in an insurance company on Shirley Avenue. He was close friends with Meyer Lansky and Joe Linsey; they had worked together as bootleggers during Prohibition. To the average citizen, he was a real estate speculator and philanthropist. But in reality, business owners paid Fox a percentage of their criminal earnings for the right to operate in Revere and guaranteed police protection. Fox had the essential cops and public officials in his pocket. There was only one rule: you couldn't commit any robberies, burglaries or anything of that nature in Revere. Salvatore "Flungo" De Angelis was his bagman. Fox's right-hand man was Morris Lynch, who took care of things when Fox was out of town or busy. Patriarca was a silent partner with Fox. He would pay Patriarca a percentage of the profits, and in return Fox was shown respect and he could go to Patriarca with any problems he may have had. When Fox died, Patriarca took the whole thing over.

Along Broadway, legitimate businesses were being operated by mid- to high-level factions of the Patriarca family. On the south end of Broadway was the Speakeasy Pub, owned by Charlie Lightbody, whose brother-in-law was Sal De Angelis. Sal was allegedly a bookmaker and loan shark who used to operate out of the pub. Sal was married to Jerry Angiulo's niece. Just a block or so up the street was Reardons Restaurant and Bar. This facility was owned and operated by the Reardon family. The current chief of Revere Police, Terrence Reardon, had to give up his silent partnership with his brother in the bar due to the bar's less-than-stellar reputation. The bar was known to have illegal gaming machines and allegations that drug dealing were taking place inside. In fact, the Reardon family was related to Charles Stuart, who was accused of killing his wife and unborn baby and blaming the incident on an African American man. The bar has since been closed and seized by the IRS for back taxes. Farther down the street was Fat

Richie, who ran a cab stand and trinket store filled with swag. Richie also used to cash checks for residents of the neighborhood and take 15 percent as his fee. Across from him was City Taxi, which was owned by Tony Defeo. Defeo was a bomber pilot in World War II and a close personal friend of Angiulo since they were kids growing up in the North End. The stand was originally a front for bookmaking, loan sharking and illegal gambling, until the cabs began bringing in more money than the illegal activities. Then there was Roy's Coin Shop, another front for bookmaking and swag. Even certain members of the Revere Police force used to sell stolen merchandise and purchase it from Roy. Roy's stepson, Joe Porter, went to school and hung around with Gigi and his family. On the northern end of Broadway was another cab stand owned by Fat Pat, another bookmaker, and farther down from him was the Pick and Save, which was owned and operated by Gigi's brother Eddie during the 1990s. An unmarked FBI surveillance car would cruise up and down this street all day long snapping pictures of the different factions and their crews. During the late 1950s and early 1960s, anyone wanting to open a cab stand in Revere had to have permission from the Angiulo family to do so.

The deputy chief of the Revere Police, Phillip Gallo, was the main protector of the mob in Revere. He had been on the pad since the days

This cab stand was owned by Tony Defeo. It was from this location that they handled illegal gambling and bookmaking operations with the Angiulo brothers, until the cabs started making more money than the illegal activities. The stand is located on Broadway, Revere, between the central fire station and Walgreen's parking lot.

Deputy Police Chief Phillip Gallo, who was on the mob payroll for most of his career. *Courtesy of Mickey Casoli.*

of Lou Fox, and after Fox died, Gallo was paid by Patriarca loyalist Maxie Baer. Gallo had a plan to take over the entire city of Revere. He set up a meeting with Henry Tameleo. The two of them met in a parking lot in Revere that was monitored by the FBI. Gallo informed Tameleo that he was planning to leave the police department and he could guarantee a wide-open town for the mob. What he needed was the backing of the mob and more money. Tameleo told him that his job was to protect the gambling, loan sharking and nightclub operations. He went on to say that the only way he was going to quit his job was if he died or was too old to work.

Off Broadway, there were at least a half dozen made members of organized crime who lived within a mile radius of one another. There was also a social club on Squire Road aptly named the Revere Businessman's Association, which was owned by Billy Baliro. During the heyday of Revere Beach, there was a supper club, which later became a strip club, named the Surf. This popular club was owned by the DiCarlo family and was used as a front for bookmaking and loan sharking activities. This club was also the site of a botched hit on Joe DiCarlo's son, which was foiled by off-duty Revere Police detective Mickey Casoli. Directly on the beach near Revere Street was the Ebb Tide, a gathering place for all the local rogues. About two blocks up from the Ebb Tide was the Mickey Mouse, a local bar that was the scene of a horrific double murder that took place right before closing. At the end of the beach is a stately home with a carriage house in the rear. The house was once home to Tommy Cerracola and his family before he was brutally murdered in the kitchen for withholding tribute on a drug deal.

Another mob hangout in Revere was Arthur's Farm, a dilapidated roadside stand that was owned by Arthur Ventola, who was a convicted fence, and his brother, Nicholas "Junior" Ventola. The roadside stand was a

Revere Police headquarters.

dumping ground for stolen merchandise; even *Life* magazine did an article about how New England Patriots players like Gino Cappelletti would shop there. It also mentioned Bob Cousy, who was the top star of the Boston Celtics. *Life* magazine made a big deal about how Cousy was friends with alleged mobster Francesco Scibelli, aka Frankie Skiball, a member of the Vito Genovese family. *Life* magazine was trying to imply that Cousy and Cappelletti were giving the mob insider information concerning professional games to make money. Nothing has ever been substantiated, and the mob has denied that any information was ever given to them. The stand was also an inconspicuous place to hold mob conferences. The stand was occasionally raided by the Massachusetts State Police but almost never bothered by the Revere Police.

The worst scandal in Revere Police history became known as the "Exam Scam." In 1987, several members of the Revere Police force paid to get the answers to the sergeant's exam. These corrupt officers took the test and memorized the answers. The test should take a minimum of four hours. The cheating officers all had an average exam time of two hours and several minutes. Once the test was turned in, the officers thought that they may be under suspicion, so they devised a plan. They came up with the bright idea to break in to where the tests were stored and change their answers to some of the questions, thinking that their test results should not be so good as to raise suspicions but only high enough to pass and be promoted. Edward Robinson, a former Revere Police officer, was found guilty of mail fraud in attempting to buy a copy of the sergeant's exam. Former Revere Police Chief John "Jake" DeLeire was also implicated in the exam fraud and convicted. After the men were caught, prosecuted and convicted, the U.S. Federal Appeals Court held up all the convictions of the seven other men, including the mastermind of the swindle, Gerald Clemente.

Another event that left a black eye on the Revere Police Department was when several officers responded to an alarm at CVS store and pharmacy on Squire Road. When the officers arrived, they noticed that the store had been burglarized. Some of the officers began filling the trunks of their police cars with merchandise from the CVS store. The corrupt officers were caught on surveillance cameras and prosecuted for their actions.

A former Revere Police officer tells a story of when he first joined the force, back in the 1950s, and he was walking a beat in Beachmont Square. This officer was filling in for the regular officer, who was on vacation. While patrolling the square, he was to call in to the station from a call box every hour after doing his rounds. When the officer went to call in to the station, he unlocked the call box and discovered a bottle of Irish whiskey inside. As the day progressed, the rookie officer took a sip of whiskey every time he called the station. At the end of the week, the bottle was gone. When the veteran officer came back from vacation, he instructed the rookie to replace the bottle and never let it happen again. This was the way the Revere Police conducted itself for close to fifty years. While these incidents do not speak well of them, the Revere Police officers were still held responsible by the general public to keep the peace. In addition, that meant dealing with the mob as part of their duties.

In September 1991, Revere Police responded to a call at a home on Mountain Avenue. There they found a pool of blood and brain tissue on the front porch. A short time later, Robert Donati was found in the trunk of his 1980 Cadillac on Savage Street. He had been bludgeoned to death and his throat was slit. Donati was a small-time racketeer who collected money for Vinny "the Animal" Ferrara, who was imprisoned at the time. At first, investigators believed that Donati was about to flip and that was the reason behind his murder. It was later alleged that Donati had been involved with the Isabella Stewart Gardner Museum Heist. In the early morning hours of March 18, 1990, two men dressed as Boston Police officers approached the museum. The museum security allowed them in but quickly realized that they weren't really cops. The infiltrators tied up the security guards and proceeded to rob the museum. Within ninety minutes, they had stolen several works of art, including Rembrandt's only seascape. They cut the works of art out of the frames, leaving only jagged edges. Investigators looked into the possibility that the IRA might have been involved with the help of Whitey Bulger. Then a small-time hood and wannabe singer named Myles Connor became a possible suspect. Although he was serving a fifteen-year sentence in a Rhode Island prison at the time of the robbery, all roads seemed to lead to him as being the mastermind behind the heist. It seems that Myles Connor and his band, the Wild Bunch, had played many clubs at Revere Beach that were frequented by Donati and other mobsters. During this time, Connor cased the Gardner Museum and informed Donati of how he could potentially commit the robbery. This very scenario may be why Donati was killed. From the 1960s until the mid-1990s, if anyone was purchasing a used car in Revere, it was best to check the trunk first.

Another incident occured at 115 Suffolk Avenue in Revere, a home that was once owned by Samuel Granito, a capo with the Angiulo faction. He was convicted of procuring the services of Frederick Simone to kill Angelo Patrizzi. After Patrizzi was found hogtied and strangled to death in the trunk of his car, FBI wiretaps picked up this conversation between Larry Zannino and Ralph Lamattina.

Zannino: "They got him. Freddy was scared to death. The kid would have clipped him in two fucking minutes."

Lamattina: "He wanted to clip Freddy. The kid wanted to ahhh."

Zannino: "Freddy fucked him in the ass."

The Patrizzi hit stemmed back to 1978, when Joseph Patrizzi, a loan shark, was shot and killed in Revere. The killer was never found but was believed to be Connie Frizzi, another loan shark who shared the same territory as Patrizzi. The mob feared that Joseph's brother Angelo, who was incarcerated at the time, would seek revenge upon his release. Angelo had other plans to revenge his brother's death. Angelo escaped from prison, and law enforcement placed several wiretaps in mob hangouts. They produced several conversations on the subject of how to kill Angelo. There was talk of offering the contract to Whitey Bulger, but Angiulo decided that it would be better to have Frizzi do it. Angelo placed a call to Roy's Coin Shop in Revere that set up the events that led to his own demise. On March 11, 1981, nine people, including Frizzi, showed up at the Harbour House on the Lynnway in Lynn to tie Angelo up and let him slowly strangle to death in his trunk in the parking lot.

Another wiretap in Lynn was placed in Studio IV, which was unofficially owned by Jerry Angiulo. It was a dance club that held monthly Las Vegas nights that would supposedly donate the house takes to charity. However, the donations were never received. One night, the FBI picked up that Jerry was passing on some fatherly advice to his son Jason on a wiretap.

Jerry: "We're talking craps now."

Jason: "Mister Vardie is my…"

Jerry: "Fucking, mother fucking big mouth cock sucker, shut up."

Jason: "You gonna listen to me?"

Jerry: "No, you mother fucker. Now shut up. Let me tell you something huh. I've been in the crap business when you were, weren't even born, you cock sucker that you are. Don't you even, ever ask me ever that a pair of dice that's been used more than one and a half or two hours without replacing it, with a brand-new set, and that set goes in your pocket and they're down the fucking sewer. Do you understand that? That's a fucking order because you're a fucking idiot. Now shut up."

Jason: "Yeah, let me tell you."

Jerry: "You talk and I'll hit you with a fucking bottle."

Now that sounds like a quality conversation between a father and son.

Mafia violence could spill over anytime, anywhere, no matter how sacred the occasion. On January 30, 1980, both Jerry Angiulo and his underboss, Larry Zannino, were attending the wedding of Bruno Balliro when Ronald Davis, another wedding guest, insulted Zannino. Consequently, Davis received a beating at the wedding. A taped conversation on March 23, 1981, revealed the circumstances of Davis's apparent suicide in his cell at Walpole State Prison.

Zannino: "You were at the wedding. You know the kid that threw a punch at me? Remember we kicked him all over the joint."

Angiulo: "You mean Liz's cousin?"

Zannino: "I had him killed in Walpole. I sent a fucking word in…he was killed in Walpole."

Angiulo: "You had the right, because [inaudible]."

Zannino: "Embarrass me in front of, he was yelling our names out… Davis."

Gigi Portalla had been exposed to this world. No matter how hard his mother had tried to protect and insulate her children from the outside world, this influence was still able to penetrate because Revere has a feeling of family. These are people you have grown up with and attended school with. In that kind of environment, it is impossible to betray old friends, no matter what they do for work.

The sweeping indictments and ultimate convictions of the men who ran the New England mob left the underworld infrastructure in complete and total chaos. Jerry Angiulo and his brothers were arrested in 1983 and convicted solely on 850 hours of audiotape that were recorded on a FBI wiretap in his office on Prince Street. Raymond Patriarca Sr. died in July 1984, leaving his son, Ray Jr., in charge. Within a few years, he found himself under indictment and ultimately convicted and sentenced to a federal prison. This turn of events caused Ray Jr. to step down as boss of the family. Ray Jr. had informed the capo regimes that in the event of his imprisonment, his successor would be Frank "Cadillac Frank" Salemme. This decision caused a major rift between the capo regimes. In early 1989, Capos Joseph A. Russo, Vincent "the Animal" Ferrara and Robert F. Carrozza broke ranks from Ray Patriarca Jr. They decided to take out Salemme before Patriarca was convicted. Since this was a risky move, they would have to assemble a crew consisting of those who were not yet made men and extremely loyal to their side. This hit was unsanctioned and would have serious consequences and repercussions if it failed. The local bosses who recruited Gigi promised to initiate him into Russo's crew as a made man if the hit was successful. This was a sign of how desperate the mob had become for new blood. Thirty years previous, this type of deal would have been unheard of.

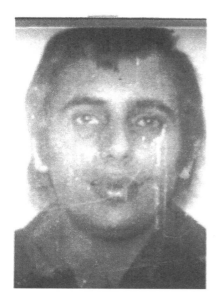

Above, left: Raymond Patriarca Jr., successor of his father. He stepped down after a few years on the throne. *AP worldwide.*

Above, right: Cadillac Frank Salemme, the former boss of the New England mafia and Gigi's nemesis. *AP worldwide.*

In the mid-afternoon of June 16, 1989, four men in black camouflage were waiting in a car outside of an International House of Pancakes in Saugus. These men were Enrico Ponzo, Gigi Portalla, John "Smiley" Mele and another man. Salemme pulled up in the parking lot in a black BMW with a briefcase containing $12,000. As Salemme attempted to exit the vehicle and head into the restaurant, the would-be assassins sprung into action. They ran up to Salemme, firing a hail of bullets. Salemme was hit twice, once in the leg and again in the chest. He managed to dodge the rest of the small arms fire and ran to the parking lot of a nearby Papa Gino's pizzeria, collapsing on the floor of the restaurant. The shooters drove away in a Chrysler. Salemme was taken to the AtlantiCare Hospital in Lynn, Massachusetts. While recovering from his wounds, he was protected by the Massachusetts State Police.

In the hours after the shooting, the police began to sweep the homes and hangouts of the usual suspects. At the border of Chelsea and Revere, police spotted Frank Imbruglia, a driver for one of the bosses. They tailed him to Gigi's home in Revere, where he entered the home and then left because

Gigi wasn't there. Nine hours after the shooting, Imbruglia drove to the Kentucky Fried Chicken in Everett and went out back. There, police found Gigi wearing a baseball cap with the Boston Police logo and a windbreaker covering a bulge in his waist. The bulge was a semiautomatic pistol that ballistic testing linked to the Salemme hit. Also present was John Mele, a small-time drug trafficker, and another man. Police also found in Imbruglia's pocket a slip of paper with a license plate number and a description of the Chrysler New Yorker that was seen by witnesses. The Chrysler New Yorker had been stolen from a rental agency where J.R. Russo's girlfriend worked. Lieutenant Charlie Quintina was waiting at the wrong restaurant for Salemme.

Gigi was held on a gun charge in Plymouth, where he shared a cell with Capo Vinnie Ferrara, who had given him the contract on Salemme. Ferrara is a Boston College graduate who, according to one affidavit, was involved in a dozen killings. Prosecutors felt that they didn't have enough evidence to charge the four men with attempted murder. However, Gigi was convicted on weapons possession and served thirty months in Leavenworth Federal Prison. Whenever Gigi was asked what Frank Salemme looked like, he would answer, "I don't know what he looks like but I sure know what he looks like running." A sense of humor and a deadly lifestyle—these are two of the traits that made up the life of Gigi Portalla.

CHAPTER 5

IRISH GANG WAR

As in other major cities, the Boston underworld was not always solely ruled by the Italian mob. The Irish had staked out a piece of the proverbial pie early on and had managed to hang on even while the Italian mob grew in power. The Irish stronghold was in the part of Boston known as Southie. This area was highly segregated and held true to its Irish Catholic heritage. Southie was one of the poorest sections of Boston and had an extremely high unemployment rate right up until the beginning of World War II. The families who lived in this tightknit community held closely to the teachings of the Catholic Church. Most of the men in Southie worked on the docks, while their wives cleaned offices in the financial district just over the bridge. Southie considered itself a closed community to everyone except the Irish. This cohesive mentality was forged when the Irish first came to Boston in large numbers and were faced with NINA (No Irish Need Apply) signs. These signs limited opportunities for Irish immigrants and only helped to reinforce the separatist attitude of this section of Boston.

Southie was under the total control of renowned gangster James "Whitey" Bulger. He arrived in Southie in 1938 with his parents and siblings. They moved into the projects, and Whitey quickly adapted to the gang life as a young man. He joined the Shamrocks, a Southie group that succeeded the former Gustins gang. The Gustins should have been the dominant gang during the Prohibition era. However, in 1931, they attempted to gain total control of Boston by taking over bootlegging operations along the waterfront.

Whitey Bulger, the kingpin of the Irish mob, who is still on the run. *Courtesy of the FBI.*

When two members of the ill-fated Gustins went to dictate the new terms to the mafia in the North End, they were gunned down behind the door of the C&F Importing Company. This single act of violence realigned the demarcation point of Boston's underworld. The Italian mafia would survive and flourish in the Italian neighborhoods, and the Irish gangs would retreat to the safety of Southie. The Irish gangs managed to survive and coexist with the Italian mafia by putting mafia loan shark money out on the streets of Irish neighborhoods.

Whitey moved quickly through the ranks of the gang by first selling swag out of the back of trucks and committing bank robbery. Eventually, Whitey was sentenced to a federal prison term. While he was incarcerated, he was moved from Atlanta to the maximum-security prison known as the "Rock." During his tenure in Alcatraz, he spent some time in solitary for fighting and organizing a work stoppage. Eventually, he quieted down and became a model inmate. When Bulger went to prison, Eisenhower was newly elected; when he was released, Lyndon Johnson was in office. While Whitey was incarcerated, his father passed away. When Whitey was released, he returned to Boston, where his brother Billy was serving a term in the Massachusetts legislature. Billy Bulger would stay in Massachusetts politics, eventually serving as the longest-running president of the chamber. Bulger later served as president of the University of Massachusetts. The post-Alcatraz Bulger quickly realized that his brother Billy's newly elected position could only benefit his climb to power.

In 1972, Whitey Bulger was working as a bodyguard for Southie bookie Donald Killeen. Bulger began to have misgivings about Killeen. He decided that he would either enter into an alliance with the Italian mob, which he distrusted and hated, or forge an alliance with the Winter Hill Gang of Somerville. Bulger knew that if he did not ally himself, he may end up dead due to Killeen's rival, the Mullin gang. Therefore, with his pride set aside, Bulger set off to see Howard "Howie" Winter. His gang was operated out of Marshall Motors in Somerville, a nondescript garage. Howie Winter associated with people like Fat Al Samenza at the Suffolk Downs Racetrack. Samenza worked in the Spit Box, which was the area of the track that tested the winning racehorse's urine. The mob would often drug horses with speed, thus the testing requirement. Samenza would switch the dirty urine with clean urine, for a price. Sometimes the mob would also pay a jockey to run interference and box other horses out as added insurance. Shortly after Bulger sided with Howie Winter, a contract killer completed a hit on Donald Killeen outside of his home. Bulger would now have South Boston, and Winter would have Whitey.

The Winter Hill Gang was started by Irishman James Buddy McLean. He was born in 1929 out of wedlock to a wealthy land speculator and one-time heir to the *Washington Post* newspaper, James McLean, in Somerville, Massachusetts. McLean was orphaned at an early age and adopted by a Portuguese family. He worked as a longshoreman on the docks of East Boston and Charlestown as a teenager. Due to his position as a longshoreman, he became a close friend of William J. McCarthy, who would later become president of the International Brotherhood of Teamsters. In 1955, McLean married a Portuguese girl and began to slowly amass a formidable criminal organization. McLean was considered one of the toughest street fighters in Boston and was well known in underworld circles. A close friend once said, "He looks like a choir boy but fights like the devil." Over the years, all his fighting took a toll on his body; he had several scars on his neck and a badly damaged left eye.

A milestone in New England gang violence began with a moment of lustful misjudgment. This lapse in judgment sparked a shooting and stabbing war among the gangs that lasted for years and strongly contributed to the eventual crippling of organized crime in the Boston area. In September 1961, two Winter Hill associates and their friend, twenty-two-year-old Charlestown mobster George McLaughlin, rented a cottage on Salisbury Beach for a Labor Day party. McLaughlin was drinking heavily throughout the day. In the evening, he attempted to grope the girlfriend of Alexander "Bobo" Petricone, who later went by the name Alex Rocco when he became an actor having a bit part in the film *The Godfather*. This single action and lapse in judgment was the catalyst that set off one of the biggest mob wars in Boston history. The two men confronted McLaughlin and gave him a savage beating. Unsure whether he was still alive, they dumped him at a nearby hospital and left to tell their boss McLean what had transpired. McLean absolved them from any wrongdoing and informed the men that he would smooth things over with George's brother, Bernie.

This was not to be; Bernie wanted revenge for what had happened to his brother, and he wanted McLean to help set up the two men responsible for the near-fatal beating. McLean was outraged and told Bernie that his brother had been out of line and had the beating coming to him. McLean stormed out of the sit-down refusing to comply with the request. Later that night, McLean awoke to the sound of his dogs being aroused and barking. As he walked to his window to see what the commotion was, he saw two men under his car. McLean, who was known for his volatile temper, ran outside firing his .38 revolver wildly at the men. The men escaped, but he found plastique explosives wired to the ignition of his car. Immediately, he suspected the McLaughlin brothers, a gang from Charlestown, and he began stalking Bernie McLaughlin throughout that neighborhood.

Bernie McLaughlin had been a loan shark and enforcer for Angiulo before breaking away and forming his own gang. With the help of his brothers, George and Edward—whom they called Punchy because of his past experiences as a boxer—he was successful in taking over the rackets in and around Charlestown. As their reputation grew, so did the requests for their assistance in contract killings. They were hired various times to perform freelance work for the Winter Hill Gang and the Patriarca family.

McLean decided to finally hit Bernie McLaughlin on his home turf: City Square, Charlestown. In broad daylight in front of one hundred witnesses, on October 31, 1961, Bernie was gunned down. Also at the scene, McLean was in a car with passenger Alexander "Bobo" Petricone, driven by Russell Nicholson. Nicholson was a member of the Winter Hill Gang and a former MDC (Metropolitan District Commission) police officer. Locals used to say that MDC stood for "more dumb cops." McLean was arrested and tried for the murder of Bernie; however, the prosecution could not find a single witness to testify as to what had occurred in Charlestown that day. McLean was acquitted of the murder charge but was convicted for illegal possession of a firearm and sentenced to two years in prison. Russell Nicholson was kidnapped and killed in 1964 by George and Punchy McLaughlin as retribution for participating in the killing of their brother Bernie. The Winter Hill Gang had attempted several botched hits on Punchy's life. During these attempts, he had lost a hand and half his jaw. After surviving the many assassination attempts, he was finally shot dead at a bus station in West Roxbury on the way to his brother George's murder trial.

Around this time, the Boston newspapers were speculating that the war between the gangs was really over the unfound Brinks Building robbery money. It was believed that some of the money may have been on ice in a warehouse near the docks of Charlestown, but this was never confirmed.

The Brinks robbery was committed on January 15, 1950, in the North End of Boston. Brinks had a garage on the corner of Prince Street, right down the street from where Angiulo would be setting up his headquarters in a few years. The garage was the central location for Brinks to bring and distribute all the money it had collected from the Boston area. About 7:30 p.m. on that January day, several men entered the building and, with precise movement, tied up the few employees who were there and proceeded to empty the vault and make their escape onto the streets of Boston. The men were all dressed as longshoremen, in knit caps and navy peacoats. The only evidence that remained was the rope used to tie up the employees and a chauffeur's cap. The police immediately began rounding up and questioning the local ex-cons and thugs, but it was to no avail. In February, several guns that were taken from Brinks employees during the robbery were found on the banks of the Mystic River in Somerville by some kids. The total haul was $1,218,211.19 in cash and another $1.5 million in checks, money orders and other securities. The press billed the heist as the crime of the century. At the time, it was the largest heist in United States history. Later, it was discovered that the men had cased the garage over the course of several years, since 1948 in fact, and had made keys to every door they needed to open. Not to mention they had gone in and out of the building several times to learn the layout.

In June 1954, one of the top suspects, Specs O'Keefe, was driving in Dorchester, Massachusetts, when a car pulled alongside his and sprayed his car with bullets. He was able to escape unscathed. Nine days later, there was another incident when O'Keefe got into a shootout with Henry Baker, another suspect in the robbery. Then, Elmer "Trigger" Burke, a professional hit man, was given the assignment to get rid of O'Keefe. The fact that Burke was hired implies a possible mob connection. His attempt went a little better: he hit O'Keefe in the wrist and chest. Burke was arrested later that day with a machine gun that ballistics was able to match to the attempted assassination of O'Keefe.

By 1956, O'Keefe cracked and told the FBI everything. Another unexpected break in the case came in June 1956. The Baltimore Police Department came across a Boston man whom they originally suspected of passing counterfeit bills. The man was registered under a fake name at a hotel. A search of his room revealed $3,780 of the Brinks money. Further conversations with the man revealed that he had a lengthy rap sheet and had recently been released from a federal prison camp. The FBI also discovered that the man was a mob associate. The man then explained that the money had been given to him by an acquaintance with whom he shared office space in Boston, a man he knew only by the name Fat John. Secret Service and the Boston Police helped to find this man. A search warrant was obtained and executed on the office, located on Tremont Street in Boston. The FBI found a partial wall, and once the partition was removed, they discovered a picnic cooler within the wall. Once they opened it, they discovered more than $57,700 in Brinks money wrapped in plastic wrap and newspaper. Further investigation revealed that the carpenter who installed the partial wall had done the work only a few weeks earlier and the cooler wasn't there at the time. The money was found to be in various stages of decomposition, which made counting the money difficult. Fat John took a plea agreement for the Brinks money that was found in his office. He served two years under the agreement.

In 1958, while out on an appeal in a narcotics case, he was found shot to death in his car, which had crashed into a truck in Boston. Police believed that Fat John was a mob associate and that his death was related to the Brinks money, although they could never prove this theory. It is highly unlikely that the heist was committed without the knowledge of the Italian mob or that they did not receive a piece of it, especially since Angiulo fenced the money years later from the Plymouth Train Robbery. Nothing went on in the North End that the mob didn't know about or allow to take place.

In the wake of the Apalachin summit, the FBI began its pursuit of organized crime. Apalachin was a meeting of all the top mobsters in the country in 1957. These men were meeting to discuss how they were going to carve up the United States among the crime families, and they anointed Vito Genovese as the boss of bosses. Unfortunately, two New York State troopers crashed the party and consequently brought the mafia into the public forefront. The FBI began bugging mob hangouts in order to obtain as much information on their illegal activities as possible. They also began working on developing informants out of current mobsters.

Originally, Patriarca stayed out of the Irish gang war. But eventually, he had no choice but to interfere because it was starting to cut into his business. His first thought was to let them kill one another, thereby allowing him to pick up a bigger piece of the pie. For the first few years, this plan worked out to his liking. As the war increased, people became increasingly outraged by the killings that were being exclaimed on the front page of the newspapers. Patriarca decided that he would use the gang war to settle some personal scores. The first score he was to settle was with Paul Colicci. They had originally been very close friends—until Colicci went to jail. While in prison, he wrote several nasty and threatening letters to Patriarca. Once released, he took up with a minor thief named Vincent Bisesi. In 1964, the two men were hustling stolen televisions in beach areas like Revere. They would use an actual TV and plug it in to show the potential customer how it worked. Then they would go out to the truck and get a new TV in a box. Unbeknownst to the customer, the set in the box didn't have any internal working parts. Patriarca found out that Colicci was living in a motel in Quincy, so he dispatched his best assassins. Unfortunately, Bisesi was there too. Patriarca's assassins killed both of them and dumped the bodies in the trunk of a car, which they left in a parking lot. The police found them on July 23, 1964, only because someone complained about the stench around the vehicle.

The second man on Patriarca's list was a minor thief named Robert Palladino. Palladino had done a burglary with Tony Sasso, in which they had broken into a house and stolen some mink coats. It turned out that the coats belonged to the girlfriend of Mike Rocco, another mob figure. The thieves sold the coats to Ralph Lamattina, another wise guy and fence. When Lamattina found out where the coats had come from, he immediately dispatched a couple of assassins. Palladino was badly beaten and then was shot and dumped in the North End in November 1965. Sasso's body was never found. It is widely believed that his remains are part of the foundation of the Wellington Shopping Center.

Meanwhile, the war between Somerville's Buddy McLean and the McLaughlin gang raged on. One evening in 1965, Buddy McLean was at the Peppermint Lounge in Somerville with bodyguards Americo "Rico" Sacramone and Anthony "Tony Blue" D'Agostino. Stevie and Cornelius Hughes opened fire as Buddy left the lounge, killing him instantly. Cornelius "Connie" Hughes was one of the most feared assassins from Charlestown and a loyal member of the McLaughlin gang. On the evening of May 26, 1966, while driving in a Revere neighborhood, he was spotted by "Cadillac" Frank Salemme and Joseph Barboza. The two Winter Hill killers pulled up to Hughes and opened fire on him. They poured round after round into his body before driving off. When the Revere Police arrived, they found a piece of Hughes's brain on the floor of his car. Revenge was sweet for the Winter Hill Gang.

After Buddy McLean was killed, Howie Winter was named as his successor. Winter was born on March 17, 1929, in Roxbury, Massachusetts. While he was still an infant, his family moved to Somerville. He began his criminal life early on and quickly became the right-hand man of Buddy McLean. He served as boss of the Winter Hill Gang from 1965 to 1978, when he was jailed for fixing horse races. The original indictment that had jailed Howie Winter also named Whitey Bulger and Stephen Flemmi. However, FBI agent John Connolly had convinced federal prosecutor Jeremiah O'Sullivan to remove them from the indictment because of their status as informants against the mafia. A few years after Winter was released, he was arrested again, this time for dealing cocaine. Despite being faced with another decade behind bars at the age of sixty-five, he refused the FBI deal, telling the agents that he was not about to be a rat. Winter was finally released in 2004 and lives somewhere in Massachusetts.

During the mob wars of the 1960s, the city of Revere was a virtual dumping ground for the bodies of those killed. With nightclubs and strip clubs dotting the city, Revere was a frequent hangout for these mobsters. One night, Revere Police officers were called to one of the clubs on the beach on the report of a shooting. Once the officers arrived, they discovered that not only was there no body, but a section of the carpet, presumably covered in blood, was missing and had been cut from the floor. Another time, the Revere Police responded to a stabbing call at a club on the beach. After arriving at the scene, the police went to inspect the bathroom only to find that the walls and floor had been conveniently cleaned.

The most famous hit man during this time was Joseph "the Animal" Barboza, who hailed from New Bedford. Barboza had been in and out of reformatories since the age of twelve. He started out as a boxer and quickly climbed the ranks of the New England mob, although he was of Portuguese decent. Barboza was with a crew out of East Boston and deferred to the Patriarca crime family and Stephen Flemmi, who was with the Winter Hill Gang. After the incident with Richard Castucci, which allowed the mob to take the Ebb Tide, Henry Tameleo spotted an opportunity. Barboza became a partner in the protection rackets. He would receive 25 percent of the profits of every club he was able to shake down for money. He and his crew were sent to over twenty clubs, including Alfonso's Lonely Hearts Club in Revere and the Frolics, which Anthony Della Russo, aka Chickie Spar, owned and operated.

Another murder that Barboza committed was the killing of Joseph Francione. Francione and Joe Puzzangara were working out a deal to purchase a load of hijacked furs from a kid named Johnny Bullets. Francione would take the furs, sell them to a guy in New York and rip off the kid Bullets. Once he discovered that he was being swindled, Bullets couldn't kill the two of them himself; however, his close friend, Joe Barboza, could. So Barboza showed up at Francione's house on South Avenue in Revere and shot him dead. The police found the body face-down in the kitchen with two shots through the back of the head.

By 1966, Barboza had worn out his welcome; he was a cold-blooded, calculated killer who now had the mob worried due to his rogue ways. In fact, he had gone into the Mickey Mouse, a bar on Revere Beach, to kill a member of the McLaughlin mob on November 15, 1965. When Barboza entered the bar near closing time, it was empty. Barboza killed Ray Distasio, a bartender, and then killed a patron who had surprised him by coming into the bar to buy a pack of cigarettes at the wrong time. The man he killed was John O'Neill, a civilian with a bunch of kids and no attachment to any mob. This type of behavior angered the bosses since dead civilians and unauthorized killings bring unwanted heat.

In October 1966, Barboza was arrested in Boston's infamous Combat Zone on a concealed weapons charge. His bond was set at $100,000. Barboza realized that something was up as soon as his bail was not put up immediately by Angiulo or Patriarca. Five weeks later, he was still in jail and two friends were attempting to collect the money to furnish his bail. Arthur "Tash" Bratsos and Thomas J. Deprisco Jr. had collected $59,000 when they visited the Nite Lite Café, managed by Ralphie "Chang" Lamattina,

Teddy Deegan, the man whose murder sent several innocent people to jail for over thirty years. *AP worldwide.*

to do a little fundraising. The next day, both men were found dead in South Boston from gunshot wounds to the head. The bodies were dumped in Southie to make it look like an Irish gang had killed them as part of the McLaughlin war. Not only were Barboza's pals dead, but the money was missing as well. In December, Joe Amico, another Barboza friend, was found murdered gangland style. The FBI figured that this was their chance to possibly turn Barboza.

In January 1967, following a ten-day trial, Barboza was sentenced to five years in Walpole on the weapons charge. By June, Barboza had had enough of doing time, and the mobsters in jail were probably walking away from him, knowing full well that he was a dead man. Barboza knew that if Patriarca wanted him dead, it would be easier to kill him in prison than on the street. Barboza began working with the FBI. The FBI was soon hailing him as the New England Joe Valachi. In August, he testified against Patriarca and Tameleo for conspiracy to murder in the killing of bookmaker Willie Mafeo, a Providence bookmaker, in 1966. He also testified against Jerry Angiulo, who was accused of participating in the murder of Rocco DiSeglio.

In October, six men were charged with the March 1965 murder of Edward "Teddy" Deegan. Barboza was at the Ebb Tide Lounge on Revere Beach that night when he and several friends left and returned approximately an hour and a half later. The Chelsea Police discovered the body of Edward Deegan slain gangland style in a Second Street alley. A thorough investigation was conducted by the Chelsea Police, and the case file even had a statement by Revere police officer Joe Errico, who was on detail that night at the Ebb Tide and personally identified the men with whom Barboza left. Teddy Deegan was part of a gang that was robbing Angiulo's bookies. They were all warned, and in 1964 they had a meeting with Angiulo and were told that they would be paying the stolen money back. Deegan was a member of the McLaughlins, so the warning was a courtesy to McLaughlin, since Angiulo had done business with him in the past and respected him. Deegan's partners, Edward Delaney and Harold Hannon, didn't listen to the warning and held up Angiulo bookmaker Carmen Puopolo in Everett. They broke into his home, held a gun to his head and proceeded to rob him. Hannon was later found strangled by a Chinese knot and dumped between some pier pilings at Logan Airport. Delaney was found the same day. He had been beaten unconscious and dumped in the harbor, where he later drowned. Deegan laid low for a while and then went back to robbing more bookmakers.

On March 12, 1965, Roy French contacted Deegan about a big score at the Lincoln National Bank. The others involved were Barboza, Ronnie Cassesso and Louie Grieco. The men then proceeded to break into the bank. On their way out, Barboza, Cassesso and Grieco turned their guns on Deegan. Deegan was murdered on orders from Peter Limone, Angiulo's right-hand man. In the first trial, none of the jurors found Barboza believable. The second trial was a different story. Patriarca was found guilty of conspiracy to kill Willie Mafeo, who was shot by four shotgun blasts in a telephone booth in a restaurant on Federal Hill.

The FBI kept moving Barboza to prevent the mob from getting at him. The mob even decided to send a message to Barboza through his attorney, John Fitzgerald. The attorney got in his car outside of his office on Chelsea Street in Everett. Suddenly, there was a large explosion, so immense that it blew out the windows of his office and the surrounding stores in the area. Fitzgerald survived but lost his right leg below the knee. Cadillac Frank Salemme and Stephen Flemmi were responsible for the car bomb. Flemmi informed on Salemme for the sanctioned bombing and caused Salemme to flee to Canada for a few years to avoid prosecution. Eventually, Salemme was caught and served time for his role in the bombing. In May 1968, the Deegan trial began. After fifty days of testimony and deliberations, the jury returned a guilty verdict. Found guilty and sentenced to death were Peter Limone, Louie Grieco, Henry Tameleo and Ronald Cassesso. Sentenced to life in prison were Joseph Salvetti and Wilfred Roy French. Barboza had done an impressive job and was sentenced to one year with time served. In 1969, he was released from prison and told to leave Massachusetts. Barboza managed to stay underground for approximately two years. He resurfaced in 1971 and pleaded guilty to a second-degree murder charge in California. He was sentenced to five years in Folsom Prison. Once he was released from

Folsom, the New England mob was able to track Barboza and his every move. Less than three months after his release, he was gunned down in San Francisco by Joseph "J.R." Russo.

In the late 1990s, the Boston FBI office was in shambles and under scrutiny for its handling of Whitey Bulger. The men who were convicted for the Deegan murder had always claimed that they were innocent and had been set up by Barboza. Even when Winter Hill hit man John Martorano became a federal witness, he informed a DEA agent that Barboza had admitted to framing the men convicted of the Deegan murder. "The mafia screwed me and now I'm going to screw as many of them as possible," said Barboza, according to Martorano. Obviously, he was referring to the fact that the mob had wanted him out because of his renegade behavior.

Around this same time, the Chelsea Police headquarters building on Broadway was undergoing a complete renovation. At one time, the building housed the police station and the district courthouse. In recent years, a new courthouse had been built across the street, and now the police were taking over the entire building. While construction crews were ripping up the former chief of police's office, the men found a thirty-year-old file that was hidden under the floorboards. The file was for the Edward Deegan murder. Documents in the file stated that Chelsea Police detectives assigned to the case had known the identities of the men involved with the murder within twenty minutes of receiving the case. It stated that Joseph Barboza, Stephen Flemmi, Vincent Flemmi (who died of a drug overdose in 1979) and Roy French (who was actually convicted of the crime) were all responsible for the murder. Meanwhile, Louie Grieco, Henry Tameleo and Ronald Cassesso—who were all innocent—had died in prison. Joseph Salvati and Peter Limone were released in 1997 and 2001, after serving more than thirty years in prison. The FBI had allowed two innocent men to waste away in jail and three known killers to continue to walk the streets of Boston because they were FBI informants. The FBI had even intimidated the chief of police in Chelsea into obstructing justice in order to protect its informants. This type of behavior was an ongoing practice with the Boston FBI office until it was exposed in 2000 because of agent John Connolly and Whitey Bulger.

Barboza had also testified against Bernie Zinna, another Revere mobster, concerning the killing of an ex-boxer in 1968. In April 1969, someone tried to kill Zinna with a shotgun on Route 60 in Malden, but they missed. Zinna was not so lucky on Christmas Eve in 1969, when he was gunned down on Ocean Avenue in Revere with a .38 caliber. He was shot four times in his Cadillac and left behind a widow and three children. Zinna was a low-level mobster whose only claim to fame was that he was tried and acquitted with Angiulo.

After Barboza was killed, J.R. Russo was promoted to capo. Joseph Russo was from East Boston. In the 1950s, he was employed as a taxicab driver and worked with the Taxi Cab Drivers Union in New York. His unofficial job was with the Lucchese crime family, the mob crew made famous in the movie *Goodfellas*. He served under the very powerful capo Paul Vario. Russo stayed with the Vario crew until the 1960s, when he moved back to Boston and served under the Patriarca crime family. After he killed Barboza in 1976, he returned to East Boston, took over a crew and ran most of the rackets around Eastie. Every afternoon, Russo would go into a butcher shop on Revere Street, in the shadow of Saint Anthony of Padua Catholic Church, and eat veal cutlets in the back room.

The two player-victims in this Greek tragedy against a background of violence with Italian and Irish participants were Richard and Carlton Eaton, who were born and raised in Revere. Carlton, who was always in trouble, became an associate of the Winter Hill Gang and close personal friend of Stephen Flemmi during the 1950s. On September 25, 1964, Carlton was sitting in his 1957 customized Cadillac Eldorado on Mingo Road in Malden when he was shot and killed by Stephen Flemmi. He was murdered for holding out on a mob tax that he was funneling through his successful sports collectibles store in South Boston. His brother Richie was just the opposite. He was successful in high school, accepted an athletic scholarship and moved from Revere to Ozone Park, Queens, in the early 1950s. He also attended Notre Dame University. After graduation, he began working with the garment workers' union. It was around this time that he became acquainted with Columbo crime family mobster Dominick Cersani. In 1978, Richie went into business with mob associate Jimmy Burke and was the front man for Robert's Lounge, a hangout for the Vario crew.

Mob associate Henry Hill stated that Richie Eaton was a "hustler on a grand scale." He was later involved in the 1978 Lufthansa heist and portrayed in the movie *Goodfellas* as the mobster who was discovered in the abandoned refrigeration truck in Gravesend, Brooklyn. It took four days to thaw out his body in order for the police to perform an autopsy. Apparently, Jimmy Burke had hogtied him and tortured his partner, allowing him to slowly strangle to death. Eaton's connection to Revere raises the question, did Patriarca receive a cut of the Lufthansa heist? We may never know.

These men were the major players of the Boston underworld during the time when Gigi Portalla grew up. In this environment, it was difficult to see the world through rose-colored glasses. After all, we live in a society in which profit supersedes people. Consumerism is the ethos of life. Revere was an exciting place during the 1950s and 1960s. The clubs on the beach were constantly being frequented by mobsters, hit men and heavy hitters from Boston and Providence. These men were exciting to be around and were idolized by the local kids. During this time in Revere, everyone would receive one hell of a streetwise education.

CHAPTER 6

MOB WAR

Joseph Russo, Vincent Ferrara and Robert Carrozza needed to eliminate their underboss, William Grasso. He was fifty-eight years old and known to have a close relationship with all five of the New York crime families. The FBI believed him to be the real power in New England. On June 16, 1989, William "the Wild Man" Grasso was found on the banks of the Connecticut River with a bullet in the back of his head. The attempted murder of Frank Salemme on Route 1 in Saugus took place five hours after police found Grasso's body. Law enforcement believed at first that the Genovese family had sanctioned the hit because Grasso had muscled in on some of their rackets in Springfield, Massachusetts, but this was not the case. These three capos were able to kill Grasso, but the failed attempt on Salemme, which was originally planned by Angelo "Sonny" Mercurio, caused further problems. They now had a major problem. The botched hit was unsanctioned and could now cost all three their lives. They decided to keep a low profile and hope that the hit team would not rat them out.

Everybody loves a gang war, whether via television, radio, newspapers, magazines or movies. Everybody, that is, except the gangs. While the general public finds gang wars exciting and fascinating, the gangs find them expensive and dangerous. Mob wars are caused by many things: young hotshots trying to push out older people, personal vendettas, expansion of turf. This soon-to-be war stemmed from the inevitable weaknesses that flow from bureaucratic inertia and the pursuit of self-interest. The New England mob had become lost after Patriarca Sr. died and Angiulo went to prison. The replacements lost sight of the game plan that was established by Patriarca Sr. When Salemme took power, he was out to get what he thought he was owed, and that meant increasing the street tax and alienating those soldiers who were in the trenches hustling the streets and earning day in and day out.

On October 29, 1989, the FBI secretly recorded a mafia induction ceremony. Present were J.R. Russo, Vinnie Ferrara, Bobby Carrozza, Dee Dee Gioacchino, reigning boss Raymond Patriarca Jr. and twelve other mafia made members. The induction ceremony took place in the dining room of an associate's home at 34 Guild Street in Medford. The following is a partial conversation between Raymond Patriarca, Biagio DiGiacomo, Joseph Russo, Angelo Mercurio and Vincent Federico.

Patriarca: "We're all here to bring in some new members into our family and more than that, to start maybe a new beginning. Put all that's got started behind us. 'Cause they come into our family to start a new thing with us. Hopefully, that they'll leave here with what we had years past. And bygones are bygones and a good future for all of us. I'll, and I'll greet you later."

DiGiacomo: "Can we open our [unintelligible] 'cause we should open it up."

Unidentified speaker: "Yeah, Yeah."

DiGiacomo: "*In onore della famiglia la famiglia e' aparta* [in honor of the family the family is open]. It means anybody want to say something [unintelligible]."

Russo: "Anything we want to discuss first? Any questions about anything first?"

Patriarca: "Yeah, I have something to say. Last week I met with Joe, to ah, kind of like, resolve ah, a few problems we had, and I want anybody to speak up [TV in the background] 'cause, 'cause I kind of like to resolve this. I appointed Joe, not only is he counselor, but he has the authority to more or less handle business in Boston when I leave [unintelligible] more or less like Jerry did when he was here. And this way you people go direct, and whatever decisions he goes by, I'll abide by. Completely. More or less for a dual purpose [unintelligible]. I hope we're all in agreement with that and I think he'll do a good job."

Mercurio: "Good luck, Joe."

DiGiacomo: "Good luck."

Federico: "Good luck [applause in background]."

Russo: "Will everybody that's being presented today, because it means Richie Floramo, Vinny Federico, there's Carmen Tortora, as well as [unintelligible]. Most of us know most of them, but some of us don't know any of these. Any remarks anybody wishes to [unintelligible] bring up [unintelligible]?"

In this conversation we can almost hear the tension of the internal problems through their conversation. The ceremony was part of Patriarca's ongoing effort to ease tensions between competing factions and establish a better working order in the post-Angiulo era. This ceremony was a wealth of information for the FBI; not only did they learn who the new members were, but they also learned about the unease between the factions. During this ceremony, Patriarca attempted to put the killing of Grasso and the attempted killing of Salemme in the past. In this business, there is a strong incentive to keep things running in the black. Deficits mean death, and the Patriarca family could not afford to have internal problems at this point in time. It was Patriarca's intention to attempt to smooth things over and help unite both factions. Had his father still been alive and in power, certain people certainly would have been killed. Patriarca Jr. believed that by initiating four new people into the family, this would appease the rival faction. When it was later revealed that Angelo Mercurio, Patriarca's driver, had helped bug the ceremony, this helped vindicate Patriarca as a bumbling idiot among his peers. Since the elder Patriarca died and Angiulo went to jail, the FBI had been exerting constant pressure on the New England mob, which had been bad for business and decimated the ranks of experienced mobsters. The induction ceremony was believed to be successful in uniting the two factions.

Unfortunately, the hazards of doing business in crime still encroached upon the mob. Less than a month later, in November 1989, Russo Ferrara and Carrozza were arrested and held on a federal indictment in Plymouth County Correctional Facility.

In March 1990, Raymond J. Patriarca Jr. was added as a defendant in a superseding indictment. Earlier, he had stepped down as family boss, a position he had held since July 1984, when his father died. According to Johnny "Sonny" Castagna, a FBI informant, in a 1989 meeting presided over by Joseph Russo and Carrozza they warned Patriarca to step down or he would be killed. When Patriarca gave up the position as head of the family, Nicholas Bianco replaced him. In a 1990 trial, Bianco was sentenced to eleven years on RICO charges. With the boss, ex-boss and consigliere all behind bars, Salemme was now heir to the throne, and with his crowning the power base moved from Providence back to Boston for the first time in thirty-seven years.

According to FBI sources, Frank Salemme took over the reins of the New England mob officially in September 1991. It is widely believed that Salemme held the title unofficially until the New York families could sit down together and give their official blessing on the nomination. In December of that same year, the FBI was able to tape a meeting at a Boston hotel between Salemme and Gambino family capo Natale Richichi. This meeting was set up to discuss how to possibly repair the growing rift between the feuding factions.

After that morning, it didn't take long for Salemme to start settling problems. During 1991 and 1992, six murders took place. At first, the FBI believed that they were related to regular mob business—until the Russo-Carrozza faction began to fight back. The first Salemme-sanctioned murder was on August 16, 1991. Howard Ferrini, a professional gambler, was beaten to death in his home and tossed into the trunk of his 1988 Cadillac. He and his car were found at Logan Airport five days later, dripping blood and emitting a foul odor. On October 3, restaurateur Barry Lazzarini was brutally beaten to death and found tied up in his home in Manomet. For at least a year, the killings seemed to have stopped. Then, in September 1992, Kevin Hanrahan was found shot to death in Providence, Rhode Island. A month later, Dedham Police found Rocco Scali, a North End restaurant owner, shot to death in his car in the parking lot of a pancake house. In December 1992, there were three more killings. Vincent Arcieri, another restaurant owner, was killed in the driveway of his East Boston home. Steven DiSarro, a South Boston nightclub owner, also turned up missing and was presumed dead.

The Russo-Carrozza contingent of the mafia retaliated on February 5, 1992. Gigi Portalla and Dennis Othmer, a twenty-five-year-old from East Boston, were driving on Blackstone Street at about 3:30 p.m. Gigi pulled up next to Dennis Caldarelli, who was also driving on Blackstone Street, and opened fire on him. Caldarelli abandoned his car and attempted to flee on foot through the North End of Boston. Gigi pursued him in a blue 1988 Chevy through the streets of Boston and finally caught up with Caldarelli at the corner of Fleet and Hanover Streets. Gigi hit him in the head with the 9 mm as he pulled alongside him. Then Gigi fired several more rounds as Caldarelli fled through backyards and alleyways. Later that evening, Gigi and passenger Dennis Othmer turned themselves in at the Revere Police Station. They informed the officer that they had not realized the police were looking for them until Gigi received a call from his mother. According to Gigi, his mother had seen on the evening news that the police were seeking her son. Gigi had only been out of prison for a short time when this incident occurred. He was convicted once again for pistol whipping and shooting at Caldarelli. Apparently, Caldarelli had insulted him and called him a nobody. Gigi was sent to Leavenworth for eighteen months. Here he was reunited with Jerry Angiulo and he started reading the works of Niccolo Machiavelli.

Once released, Gigi opened a restaurant in Everett. He named the restaurant Something Fishy, a sneer at local law enforcement. During this time, he and his crew also began shaking down local bookmakers along the North Shore. As Gigi grew in power, he began to diversify his criminal portfolio. His next step was to invest in the drug trade. He established a drug-selling network with "Fat" Charlie McConnell and Bobby Nogueira, an ex-con who loved drugs and violence in equal amounts. This was his crew, the men he would work with and with whom he would attempt to take over the trafficking in the Boston area. Gigi would drive around with his crew in rented Chevy Blazers. He didn't trust cars that weren't rented on the spot with no reservations. He would frisk his own friends and crew. Gigi would drive, McConnell would be in the passenger seat and Nogueira would be riding in the rear with a loaded weapon. They had a cellphone with an East Boston number, which received calls from customers around the clock. They would sell forty-dollar bags of cocaine. Charlie McConnell would have a can of soda between his legs to help him swallow the bags of coke if they were to be stopped and searched by police. In the glove box was a bottle of Ipecac to help Charlie vomit the bags up after the police left. Gigi never carried more than thirteen grams of cocaine on him, so if he was caught he couldn't be prosecuted for trafficking. At the height of his business, the crew was selling five-plus kilos a week, bringing in $20,000 a kilo. Gigi and his crew delivered coke to every bar, lounge and nightclub in Revere, East Boston, Winthrop and Chelsea. They were known as DOW: drugs on wheels.

Gigi was still having feuds with other mobsters at this time. Only now, the feuds were on a different level. One evening, Gigi was entering the tunnel in East Boston to head into Boston for a night of drinking. Another car pulled alongside his. In the car were Bobby Luisi and his son, Roman. The Luisis were well-known North End bullies. They exchanged words with Gigi, and before anyone knew what had happened, the Luisis pulled out a gun and began firing. Gigi floored his car and raced through the tunnel while trying to reach the gun under his seat. He finally reached the gun and began firing back at the Luisis. The gunfight went back and forth as the two cars barreled through the Callahan Tunnel. Neither party hit its respective target. Gigi eventually lost the father-and-son duo once they got out of the tunnel. The Luisis were later gunned down, along with two confederates, at the 99 Restaurant in Charlestown. The shooting made the front page of the *Boston Herald*. It is widely believed that the Luisis were trying to scare Gigi from encroaching on their territory in the North End.

In April 1992, Carrozza was sent to federal prison. While he was serving his time in Pennsylvania, Anthony Ciampi and Michael Romano Sr. visited him and requested permission to go to war against Salemme.

This was a period of constant reminders that the mob was ever present along the North Shore of Massachusetts. On April 2, 1993, in a Kentucky Fried Chicken parking lot in Everett at the corner of Route 16 and Everett Avenue, a white GMC rapidly sped into the lot. Two men exited the vehicle, leaving the doors ajar. They walked toward two cars parked in front of the GMC, and each man grabbed a driver and threw him into the back of the GMC. One of the men got back into the GMC and drove off. The passenger of the GMC then got into and drove off in one of the cars that was parked in front of the Kentucky Fried Chicken. The whole incident took approximately thirty to sixty seconds. Witnesses described the driver as a twenty-year-old male who appeared

The KFC parking lot where drug dealers were abducted and Michael Romano Jr. was killed while changing a flat tire.

to have a gun. The passenger was wearing a DEA hat and a DEA jacket. Police searched the car that was left behind and discovered a kilo of 87 percent pure cocaine. Police quickly determined that this was an attempt to steal the drugs, but the robbers had driven off with the wrong vehicle. The GMC had been reported stolen by Romano about two hours before the kidnapping took place. Romano had rented the vehicle at National Rental Car at Logan International Airport. Police also believed that Romano was the man wearing the DEA apparel.

Another horrific incident took place one night when Gigi, his brother Eddie and Enrico Ponzo pulled up to a convenience store on Squire Road in Revere. The three men entered the premises and began to get a few snacks. Ponzo picked up a candy bar and began eating it in the aisle. The store clerk, a big Texan cowboy type, said, "Ya have to pay for that before you eat it." Ponzo, feeling embarrassed, went up to the counter and apologized. At the counter, he proceeded to ask the clerk how much a large metal flashlight would cost. The clerk answered his question, and Ponzo agreed to purchase the flashlight. He then asked the clerk to install the D cell batteries in it, which the clerk did and then rang up the entire purchase. Ponzo paid the clerk, and when the clerk gave him his change, Ponzo grabbed him, pulled him over the counter and began to beat him with the flashlight. Within seconds, the clerk was lying in a pool of his own blood. Eddie had to interrupt Ponzo and tell him that the cops were on the way in order to prevent him from killing the clerk. Gigi and Ponzo exited the store laughing as if they had just pulled a childish prank. That is just how quickly you can be involved in an altercation with these guys. The mob's violence does involve the public from time to time. The raw impulses that define life on the streets take over with these men, and there is only blind allegiance to the wise guy way.

Another time, Gigi and his crew needed to send a message to a person who owed him some money. Gigi came up with the idea of buying a tombstone. He placed it in the trunk of his car and drove away. Later in the evening, he took the tombstone to the man's house and proceeded to throw it through the guy's living room window. The next day, the man contacted Gigi and paid the debt in full. He had received the late payment notice loud and clear.

During this time, Gigi and his crew began hanging around at a private club located at 151 Bennington Street in East Boston. The club was in a nondescript storefront in a heavily overcrowded area of Eastie, surrounded

Left: Rico Ponzo, a cold-blooded psychopathic killer who is still on the run. *Courtesy of the FBI.*

Below: The building on the right was the social club for the Russo-Carrozza faction located at 151 Bennington Street in East Boston. The pay telephone on the building across the street was where Michael Romano Sr. gunned down one of the men he believed responsible for his son's death.

by other mom and pop stores and forbidding three-deckers. The street was constantly congested with traffic and pedestrians. This was the perfect location to avoid the incessant surveillance of the FBI and the state and local police. The pay phones on the corner also helped the local mobsters avoid telephone taps. The club was owned by Anthony Ciampi, a local bookmaker and loan shark who lived nearby. The club became known as the war room due to the amount of guns and ammo that was being housed at the location. Every so often, the FBI or local and state police would serve a warrant on the club and search it. Mostly they were looking for the occasional weapon or betting slips, or possible information about a hijacked truck of swag out of Logan International Airport.

One of the mobsters who hung around the East Boston club was Michael P. Romano Sr. A Suffolk Superior Court jury acquitted Romano of the 1993 killing of Penrod E. Lashod in East Boston. Lashod was shot to death on his boat, the *Irish Temper*. A co-defendant and one-time close friend of Romano's, David J. Boyd, testified that the killing was because of Lashod's refusal to pay rent to Romano. Boyd is now in witness protection. Prior to the acquittal, Romano had approached the Suffolk District Attorney's Office and offered to plead guilty to manslaughter, but the district attorney refused the plea.

Mark Spisak was an employee of the club as well as an associate of the men who hung out there. Spisak was a dealer for the card games at the club, which began on Friday nights and continued through Sunday mornings. He learned the illegal gambling business by the age of nine from his stepdad, who was a bookie. At age seventeen, he was working as a professional poker player. While working at the club, he made $200 to $400 in tips and $7.50 an hour. The club would rake in 5 percent of the first $1,300 of each hand. During the week, Spisak worked as a truck driver for Sky Chef at Logan International Airport. There he would load meals and liquor onto the planes prior to their departures. One time, Spisak drove his truck to the club and unloaded a full load of liquor into the club. During this time, there were other card games taking place in East Boston. Cadillac Frank Salemme had a game run by Bobby Luisi Jr.—the same Bobby Luisi who shot at Gigi—on Marginal Street, and there was also one run by the Rossettis in Orient Heights, a section of East Boston. Spisak worked as a dealer at all three clubs. Eventually, Spisak only worked for Ciampi due to the increasing friction between Ciampi and Salemme.

On the evening of March 31, 1994, Ciampi pulled up in his silver Lincoln and called for Spisak to come out of his apartment. In the front seat next to Ciampi was neighborhood kid Nick Patrizzi. Spisak came out and got into the rear of the Lincoln, and Ciampi began to drive around East Boston. Ciampi spotted Michael Rossetti and Richard Devlin walking on London Street and told Spisak to get out and shoot them. Spisak exited the vehicle and stalked them for a while until the men stopped and turned around. Spisak crossed the street and pretended to be looking in a bakery window. Then Spisak returned to the vehicle and they continued to follow Rossetti and Devlin. In the immediate area of Ciampi's club, Ciampi spotted and pointed out some men sitting in a Skylark parked in front of 25 Bennington Street. The men in the car were Michael Rossetti, Richard Gillis and Richard Devlin. Ciampi pulled alongside Devlin and yelled "Unload!" Ciampi fired his revolver five or six times, hitting Devlin in the head. Rossetti ducked down and escaped out the passenger side door while Gillis got out of the rear car door.

Spisak found that his window was up during the attack, so he cowered on the floor of the car until the shooting was over. As they pulled away, Stephen Rossetti fired two shots back at his would-be assassins. Ciampi drove down Bennington Street and pulled the car over in the parking lot outside his club. He questioned Spisak as to why he hadn't shot at the men. Spisak lied and told Ciampi that his gun had jammed. Ciampi took the gun from Devlin and fired a round into the ground. The men then proceeded to exit the vehicle and walk toward the house of Ciampi's brother, Robert "Puss" Ciampi, to get another car. They went to Paris Street, where Ciampi lived next door to his parents. After talking with his dad Louis "Jumbo" Ciampi, family friend Bobby Fawcett pulled up. Fawcett was an icon in the Boston Police Department, and after he retired he worked as head of security at Suffolk Downs. His wife Jackie was the personal secretary for Mr. Omalley, the owner of Sterling Suffolk Racetrack. Fawcett drove Spisak, Jumbo and Anthony Ciampi to a self-service gas station near Suffolk Downs, where they purchased two dollars' worth of gasoline so that Ciampi could follow Fawcett's advice to wash his hands with gasoline to remove any traces of gunpowder residue. Ciampi and Spisak decided to flee and go down to the Cape Cod cottage of Mark Ricupero, a dealer at Ciampi's card games. Nine days later, Spisak and Ciampi went to Florida and joined up with Ciampi's wife and kids in a preplanned trip. After the trip, they all returned to Massachusetts.

Boston Police arrived around 9:30 p.m. to investigate the shooting. When they arrived, they found Devlin slumped over the steering wheel of his 1994 Buick Skylark. The car was parked in front of a restaurant that was once owned by Biagio DiGiacomo, who went to prison in 1991. Devlin was wearing a bulletproof vest, had been shot in the head and was in critical condition. He died after a few days on life support in Massachusetts General Hospital. Devlin had been a brutal enforcer for Salemme. In 1971, he was convicted of manslaughter. It seems that he chopped off his victim's head, hands and right leg. The hatchet he used was found buried in the victim's chest when the corpse washed up in Dorchester Bay. While in Walpole Prison, he was a prime suspect in the 1973 killing of Albert DeSalvo, the Boston Strangler.

Two trials both ended in hung juries, and the case was never solved. He was also a suspect in the murder of Rocco Scali.

Richard Gillis approached the police investigating the scene and informed the officers that he too had been hit. He was wounded in the mouth and had been grazed slightly on the head. Gillis told police that he had not been in the vehicle but had a hard time explaining why his teeth, which had been shot out, were in the backseat. Gillis had been shot six times at close range in 1980 at Copps Hill Cemetery and was a suspect in the murder of Vincent Arcieri. Gillis and Devlin were considered Salemme's top muscle in Boston.

The same night that Devlin and Gillis were shot, Ronald Coppola and Peter Scarpellini suffered the same fate as they were playing cards in a social club in Cranston, Rhode Island. Police arrested Antonio "Nino" Cucinotta in connection with the shootings. He confessed to the murders, stating, "They failed to defend his honor when another man insulted him." Both men worked for Salemme lieutenant Robert "Bobby" DeLuca.

Law enforcement began to speculate that there was a rift between the old guard and the Salemme loyalists. They knew that the shootings weren't related yet they speculated as to the possibility that Salemme was beginning to charge a higher rate of tribute while not offering enough protection for his men.

Around this time, Eddie Portalla's good friend Joe received a call from his girlfriend, who was crying. Joe hung up with her and was immediately and visibly upset. He is a mountain of a man, standing at about six feet, three inches, and weighing in at about 350 pounds of solid muscle. Joe proceeded to tell Eddie that his girlfriend's boss had insulted her and called her a bitch. Joe felt helpless because her boss was a connected guy, and if he did anything, there would be reprisals. Eddie told him not to worry, and they loaded up a couple of cars with mob associates and proceeded to the restaurant. Once they arrived, Joe approached the boss, surrounded by a bunch of young Turks, and asked the man if he had made the comment. The boss's reply was an affirmative one, and he further stated that he would not be taking the comment back or apologizing. At that point, Joe hauled off and hit him square in the face, knocking the man out of his shoes in front of the wait staff and patrons. Joe and his gang of toughs proceeded to turn around and exit the restaurant. No reprisals ever came about due to this incident.

On July 11, 1994, John Marlon, Sean Cote and John S. Patti broke into a sandwich shop in East Boston where it was known that a couple of handguns were being kept. The trio decided that if they were going to continue going down the list of Salemme associates they wanted killed, then more guns would be needed.

In the summer of 1994, Sonny Mercurio, a member of the Carrozza faction, was arrested in Georgia on drug trafficking charges. Mercurio was a fugitive at the time and was sentenced a year later. He was a major player in the trafficking of drugs coming to Massachusetts. His arrest was a major blow to the drug trade in Boston.

Romano Jr. was driving Enrico Ponzo and Robert "the Blur" Paleo to Everett to pick up an extortion payment from Joseph Cirame, owner of the Stadium Café in Everett. Salemme loyalists learned that Ponzo was attempting to muscle in on payments that were going to them. Romano Jr. was left in the Kentucky Fried Chicken parking lot in Ponzo's girlfriend's car with a flat tire. Romano volunteered to change the tire while Paleo and Ponzo walked to the Stadium Café. While he was in the process of changing the tire, a man approached his vehicle and began kicking the tires. When Romano asked him what he was doing, the man pulled out a gun. He pressed it to Romano's cheek and pulled the trigger. Romano Jr. was killed at 9:20 p.m. on September 1, 1994. After the shooting, Everett detective Charles Marchese saw Paleo and Ponzo walking toward the Stadium Café. Later that night, he saw them in a dark-colored Cadillac driven by a third man who was believed to be Cirame. Jerry Matricia, a bookmaker, believed that Ponzo was the intended target since he was considered the most dangerous of the men who were present.

Later, Romano Sr. confided in Sean Cote and David Clark that Joseph Souza and Lonnie Hilson had killed his son. Romano had been a standout hockey player at Wakefield High School. He was married to a schoolteacher and had a small daughter. He got involved with Rico Ponzo when he was having some financial troubles. In August 1994, he and Ponzo were arrested when Boston Police witnessed Ponzo hand a bag of cocaine to someone. During the pursuit that followed, Romano was spotted throwing a bag that contained the supply of coke they were selling that night. Ponzo and Romano were supplementing their income by dealing coke and crack. Romano's family and friends were shocked by the arrest. Ponzo, on the other hand, was known by law enforcement and had been since 1986, when he supplied the guns that took the lives of two young guys in a park in the North End.

Violence at this time continued to thrive, as a day later, Massachusetts state trooper Mark Charbonnier was gunned down on Route 3 in Kingston at 3:00 a.m. during a routine traffic stop of a van driven by a paroled killer. A shootout ensued because while he was being questioned, the driver became spooked and began firing. He shot the trooper in the stomach right below his bulletproof vest. David Clark, the driver, thought that the trooper knew he had just killed Romano Jr. Charbonnier was medi-flighted to Beth Israel Hospital, where he died on the operating table. Even with his wound, the trooper was able to hit the driver in the left arm and head. After a thorough investigation, Clark was arrested and convicted of murder.

An interesting mob associate was Sean Cote. He was a polite boy until a family tragedy changed his life forever. Born in Everett, his parents divorced when he was a toddler. He and his older sister went to live with their mother Barbara, a hairdresser. At age twelve, he went to stay with his father's family. When at the funeral of his paternal grandmother, he learned that his mom had perished, at the age of thirty-four, in a North Reading house fire. The arson investigators came to the conclusion that the fire was started on the back porch by someone playing with matches. It is widely believed that Sean may have possibly started the fire by accident; however, this is only speculation. Sean moved into the Kelly's Meadow section of Revere, and shortly thereafter he began stealing cars. One day, he was driving through the Revere High School parking lot with a stolen Pontiac Trans Am. Suddenly, the car stalled. Sean proceeded to re-hotwire the vehicle right in front of a shop teacher. The car started back up and he proceeded to drive off. By age nineteen, he had been in court more than one hundred times on charges including stolen motor vehicles, breaking and entering and cocaine possession. All the while, his Bay Road neighbors loved and adored him due to his outgoing personality and willingness to assist those in need. In 1990, he crashed a stolen car into a Chelsea storefront during a high-speed chase. He was convicted of assault with intent to murder and served two years in prison. While in prison, he befriended alleged armored car robbers Matthew McDonald and Patrick McGonagle, alleged mafia enforcer Darin Buffalino and Gigi Portalla.

In August 1994, two armored car guards were slain during an $800,000 heist in Hudson, New Hampshire. Shortly after, a stolen Mazda 929 was found burning behind Johnny's Foodmaster Supermarket in north Revere. This location was a place where Sean Cote had disposed of stolen cars in the past. The Revere Fire Department found $1,000 in $1 bills in the trunk as well as a jumpsuit from the heist that was barely singed. It is widely believed that Sean was the wheelman and was not involved in the killing of the two guards. The police immediately began to search for Cote. In January, he was found holing up in a house in Revere with a gun and eighty packets of heroin. The Massachusetts State Police and the FBI surrounded the home and besieged it for several days. Later, it was discovered that Cote had made a hasty retreat a day or two before law enforcement surrounded the home.

Cote, who originally worked freelance and floated freely from one crew to the next without allegiance to any faction of the New England mob, decided to ally himself with the Carrozza-Russo faction. This decision came sometime in September after his friend, Romano Jr., was killed. Cote was considered the best wheelman in the business. Any time a stolen car or a driver was needed for a getaway, Cote's services were sought out. Now he would work solely for the Carrozza-Russo faction.

Bobby Romano Jr.'s murder created a chain of vicious events, driven by the vindictiveness of Bobby's father, Robert Sr., who was frequently at the helm.

On September 16, 1994, Paul Strazzulla was lying in wait in the driveway of Cirame's house in Revere at about 2:00 a.m. As Cirame opened the door of his car, Strazzulla, dressed in a black hood and jumpsuit, took a crouching position within five feet of Cirame and unloaded his weapon. The street and driveway began to fill with blood as Cirame was hit in the abdomen and legs, but he survived the shooting. Cote drove one getaway car while Enrico Ponzo drove the other. Romano Sr. and Ciampi provided the weapon used in the shooting. Cirame survived yet another shooting. An earlier attempt undertaken by Romano, Cote and Arciero had also failed.

On September 21, 1994, John Arciero and Sean Cote had been up for the past four days straight smoking coke in Cote's East Boston apartment. At 3:00 a.m., Michael Romano Sr. picked up Arciero to drive a getaway car for a planned hit. Michael Prochilo was the intended target because he was allied with Salemme. Prochilo had previously stolen drugs from dealers who worked for Nazzaro "Ralph" Scarpa and John S. Patti. When the hit squad approached Prochilo in his car, which was parked on Gladstone Street in East Boston, Cote leapt from the moving vehicle and began shooting at him. It was strictly amateur time; Prochilo spotted the hit squad approaching in a car and ducked to avoid injury. Cote missed him completely. Patti began to back the car up in order to pick up Cote and make their escape, when suddenly he hit Cote with the door of the moving car. Arciero, who was waiting at a location nearby in a second getaway car, left after ten minutes, probably paranoid from being high on crack. This was a procedure that was done because of witnesses seeing and being able to describe the original car. This action left Cote and Patti with no getaway car. They were forced to carjack a *Boston Globe* delivery truck to get back to Cote's apartment.

Four days later, Cote, Romano Sr., Spisak and Arciero were in a car in the parking lot of the White Hen Pantry on Maverick Street in East Boston. Romano spotted Timothy Larry O'Toole as he pulled up to the convenience store. Romano yelled out, "Get him!" Cote jumped out of the vehicle, ran up to O'Toole and stabbed him in the chest. Cote then jumped back into the car and Romano Sr. sped off. O'Toole survived the stabbing but later testified in court that he believed a stockier man than Cote had stabbed him.

Around the same time, Scarpa, Strazzulla, Cote and Paul Decologero attempted to kill Rossetti in Revere. They missed and Rossetti returned fire. However, the attempted assassination was a wash since Rossetti wasn't killed and none of the assassins was hit either.

On October 20, 1994, at about 5:20 p.m., a lone gunman crossed a busy Bennington Street in East Boston. The assassin approached Joseph Souza, who was using a pay phone located across from Anthony Ciampi's Social Club, next to Sava's Market. As pedestrians walked in every which direction on the mild October afternoon, the shooter pulled out his weapon and proceeded to shoot Souza, who was standing next to two Mormon missionaries. Souza was hit four times as he attempted to get his .45-caliber weapon out of his shoulder holster before slumping to the ground. In full view of eyewitnesses, the gunman simply slipped into the crowd and disappeared. Witnesses who were standing not more than ten feet away at the time of the shooting couldn't identify or agree on the description of the shooter. Michael Romano Sr. of Wakefield had told associates that he had killed Souza.

In late October, Cote was chased through the streets of East Boston by Salemme loyalists. When he told Ciampi about the incident, Ciampi informed Cote that if he needed any guns he could come to his club because he had them stored there.

In the fall, Eugene "Gino" Rida, Cote and Leo Boffoli, a bookmaker, sat down at a restaurant to discuss the upcoming hit on Matteo Trotto. Rida was telling Boffoli about the mob war in Boston and the ongoing battle over protection money. Rida went on to say that if the Salemme faction lost, then he would have control over Worcester. Rida used Cote's reputation as a hit man to threaten Boffoli's compliance with the plan.

On October 31, Boffoli brought Sean Cote to Worcester to help in a personal feud between Rida and Trotto. It seems that Trotto was refusing to pay protection and Rida wanted to kill him. This would serve to send a message to other drug dealers and bookies that it was in their best interest to pay the protection. Boffoli suggested that they extort Trotto rather than kill him, but Rida wanted him dead. Rida decided that Boffoli would lure Trotto to the phone booth outside the gym, and there Cote would kill him. Rida had plans of moving out to Worcester and starting to shake down bookmakers and dealers. Cote would be the bagman and Rida would be the boss. Boffoli and Rida were both bookmakers and saw an opportunity to take over Worcester. Romano was Rida's cousin, and he was being schooled by Romano in the art of loan sharking and shakedowns in an attempt to take over Worcester.

During this time, Gigi and his crew were continuing to shake down drug dealers and increasing their street prowess and bankrolls. They controlled most of the drug trade in the Greater Boston area. In fact, a safe house that Gigi was using on Shirley Avenue was raided by the Revere Police and the Massachusetts State Police. When the raiding party arrived to search for drugs, all they found was an empty safe with a Revere Police badge in it with the numbers cut off. This incident helps to exemplify how powerful Gigi was becoming. He obviously had a cop on the pad who tipped him off about the raiding party. The police badge was a slap in the face to the police serving the warrant, as if to say, "I knew you were coming."

On November 9, 1994, Boston Police arrested Joseph Calderelli, who worked for Patti and provided Matricia with drugs, at Bennington and Brooks Streets. They seized coke, heroin and a .38 handgun in the car, which was used by Calderelli and owned by Patti.

In December, Cote and Rida went to Ciampi's club and swapped a .38 handgun that wasn't working for a semiautomatic Mac 10. This is just a

The VFW club in Revere where Paul Strazzulla's body was dumped and the car was set on fire.

small peek into the number of weapons that were stored in the war room at Ciampi's club on Bennington Street.

On December 11, Anthony Diaz, Strazzulla and Ciampi were driving around East Boston late at night when Diaz pulled out a gun and shot Paul Strazzulla in the head. The men dumped the car at the Beachmont VFW parking lot on the Revere–East Boston line. Then they got into a parked car and drove away. Diaz, fearing that he had left some trace of evidence or a fingerprint that could be traced back, went and got Cote. They returned to the parking lot, and Cote set fire to the vehicle with Strazzulla's body in it. The Revere Fire Department responded to the scene and found a 1988 Oldsmobile Cutlass burning out of control. After extinguishing the fire, they discovered Strazzulla's body. He was reputed to be a close friend of Rico Ponzo. Earlier in the evening, Cote and Ciampi had gone to see Matricia, who escaped because he believed the two men had come to kill him.

On December 15, the FBI served a search warrant at 151 Bennington Street. The warrant allowed the FBI to recover ballistic evidence.

In January 1995, a federal grand jury handed down a thirty-seven-count indictment against Frank Salemme and six other members of the Boston mob. Whitey Bulger was also named in the indictment, along with Stephen Flemmi. James Ring, former supervisor of Boston's FBI organized crime squad, stated, "It's kind of a stake through the heart." It would take over five years to bring these men to trial.

Salemme went into hiding just before the indictments were announced. While on the run, he left his brother Jackie as acting boss of the family. He was eventually caught in August 1995 in West Palm Beach, Florida.

On May 17, 1995, Mark Spisak, Ciampi and Anthony Rizzo happened by chance to spot Stephen Rossetti on the highway while they were returning from a roast beef sandwich shop in Revere. Spisak, who wanted to avenge himself for failing to kill Rossetti a year earlier, offered to do the hit. They found Rossetti's van parked near his parents' home on Waldemar Avenue in East Boston. Spisak exited the vehicle and hid behind a fence with a semiautomatic weapon. The other two men were waiting approximately seventy yards away in the getaway car. In the driveway between 122 and 124 Waldemar Avenue, Spisak accidentally made a noise and alerted Rossetti as he approached. Spisak lurched out of the shadows at Stephen Rossetti and began firing at him. After the first shot, the glove that Spisak was wearing got jammed in the firing mechanism. Rossetti, stunned at first, immediately began to wrestle with Spisak. Finally, he was able to get out his gun and get off a couple of shots before making his escape. The first bullet passed clearly through Spisak's leg, another shattered his right arm and a ricochet hit him in the head. Spisak almost immediately heard sirens coming from the direction of Suffolk Downs Racetrack. Ciampi pulled up to Spisak and called out, "Oh Mark. Oh my God, Mark." Rossetti turned and ran. Rizzo was screaming at Ciampi, "Come on. We've got to get the fuck out of here."

Boston Police officer Michael Leary found Spisak walking aimlessly. A search of the area turned up a jammed semiautomatic weapon with a matching glove to the one Spisak was wearing in the grass. There was a single spent 9 mm cartridge and eleven cartridges in the magazine. Police officers also discovered five other shell casings on the ground from a different gun. Boston Police blanketed the area but were unable to turn up Rossetti. Spisak was arrested and taken to Massachusetts General Hospital. After Spisak was released from the hospital, he stayed with Anthony Ciampi and his family. While living there, he and Ciampi outlined how to get the others on a list of at least fourteen people who were strong Salemme loyalists. The group was attempting to find out through the Registry of Motor Vehicles where Rossetti lived but was unsuccessful.

Gigi was finally able to obtain the information on Rossetti's address in Revere. Romano then parked a stolen car outside of his house and placed a video camera in it to monitor his movements. He bought the camera and night vision goggles with the proceeds from marijuana that Cote, Ciampi and Arciero had stolen from a dealer and sold. Despite Spisak's performance in the two botched hits, Romano still relied on Spisak to provide security when he met Bobby Luisi Jr. inside Kelly's Pub in East Boston. This meeting was an attempt to possibly hammer out an uneasy peace or truce. It was at this meeting that Luisi informed Romano that Devlin hadn't been targeting Ciampi. Rather, when Devlin was killed he had been looking to kill Gigi. This conversation helps to show just how powerful Salemme perceived Gigi to be. The hierarchy of the New England mob believed that Gigi might someday soon make a play against them, and if successful, he would be next to take the throne. At that time, a truce was attempted to be negotiated, but it was too little too late.

During this time, Gigi and his drug network were becoming more entrenched in the New England landscape. However, Gigi was becoming increasingly more paranoid. Around this time, Gigi began to befriend a mob wannabe named Smiley Mele. In July 1996, Mele was caught with one hundred pounds of marijuana in the trunk of his car. He had a gun on him but was able to pass it off to the passenger, who subsequently went to jail for possession of a firearm. The DEA, pressuring Mele, was eventually able to turn the twenty-nine-year-old East Bostonian into an informant. Mele was able to keep his arrest from Gigi, and he began to ingratiate himself further into Gigi's close circle. Mele even went so far as to sell a $10,000 pickup truck to Gigi for $3,000. Fearing that it may have been bugged, Gigi never drove the vehicle.

On a federal wiretap, Mele attempted to get Gigi and Bobby Nogueira to discuss any criminal activity that they may currently be involved in.

Gigi: "He [Nogueira] knows where to put it, how to use it, how to move it. How long would it take you to take a head off?"

Nogueira: "With the Spider?"

Gigi: "With the Spider, sharp as a motherfucker."

Nogueira: "About a minute."

Mele: "A minute, Bob?"

Nogueira: "A minute."

Gigi: "The spine's the hardest part."

Mele then asked Nogueira if he was haunted by the memories of those he had killed.

Mele: "It doesn't, it doesn't bother ya? You don't wake up at night?"

Nogueira: "No, I relive."

Mele: "You do relive it? How? What do you do, dream about it?"

Nogueira: "It's just as good as the real thing."

Mele: "God. I couldn't do that."

Gigi: "What do you mean, you relive it?"

Nogueira: "I dream it."

Gigi: "Do you really?"

Nogueira: "Yeah."

Gigi: "You gotta love it, but that's a rare dream. That's about as rare as a wet dream. Bob, let's put it this way right? Ninety, 99.9 percent of the time it's what, well deserved, right?"

Nogueira: "Oh, maybe a hundred."

Gigi: "So there's no conscience with it because it's necessary."

Mele even pestered Gigi to sell him coke, and when he learned that Gigi was going to visit his son in Arizona, he ingratiated himself further with Gigi and the group in an attempt to go on the trip. In December 1996, Mele convinced Gigi to purchase five kilos of cocaine for $15,000, which would be shipped to him in Massachusetts. Gigi, McConnell and Mele would meet at a later date in Las Vegas and Arizona with undercover DEA agents to finalize the deal. Mele even went so far as taking Bobby Nogueira out to buy Christmas gifts for his children and paying for Nogueira's room at the Comfort Inn on his credit card. This is possibly how the hit men learned where Nogueira was staying, since he was under an assumed name.

On November 14, 1996, bloody remains were found in a Danvers, Massachusetts dumpster. At a car wash business, a man found two bloody MVP gym bags, lime and clothes in a dumpster. Police quickly linked a missing Medford woman and two deadly drug overdoses in Stoneham to a North Shore ex-con with mob ties. Originally, it was believed that the girl was killed because she was an informant who ratted on Gigi's gun-running operation; however, this was not the case. It turned out that Aislin Silva was killed because she allowed police to find a cache of high-powered weapons that a friend had stolen from Gigi. An ex-con named Kevin R. Meuse had been seen around the time of the murder with a known Portalla associate. Stephen DiCenso suffered permanent brain damage from his drug overdose and his two friends, Stephen Yorks and Paul McCarthy, both died from their overdoses. It was widely speculated that Gigi had supplied the heroin that killed them. DiCenso was ruled incompetent to stand trial and face federal gun charges. Silva was last seen with DiCenso getting into a 1991 Ford Explorer two days before her tissue was found in the dumpster along with Meuse's fingerprints. Meuse drove a 1991 Explorer that matched the vehicle's description. He had been released in 1996 from Massachusetts Correctional Institute at Cedar Junction Walpole after serving seventeen years for armed robbery and attempted murder. Meuse was working out at the time at Paul's Gym in Woburn, Massachusetts. The gym is owned by Paul DeCologero, who, with three relatives and a family friend, was facing federal drug charges. The family also has ties to Gigi.

Additionally, in December Gigi drove to New York to talk to the head of the Gambino family, the traditional ally of the Patriarca family. On the way to New York, he stopped off in Providence to visit Luigi "Baby Shanks" Manocchio, who operated out of Café Verde on Federal Hill. Salemme had installed Baby Shanks as acting head of the family while he was going through the trial for his life. Gigi cruised Atwell Avenue for at least thirty minutes searching for the café. Running late for his meeting, he gave up the search and headed to New York. For the moment, at least, Baby Shanks was still in power. The meeting with the head of the Gambino family helped to establish that Gigi was planning to make a move and was seeking permission from one of the most powerful families on the commission.

Baby Shanks Manocchio was a small man with a receding hairline and eyes of steel. He was well read, spoke several languages fluently and could be called a kind of renaissance gangster. He was even an international fugitive. He fled the country when he was indicted for his role in the murder of two renegade bookmakers in 1968. By July 1979, he was tired of running, so he returned to Rhode Island and surrendered himself. In 1983, he finally stood trial for the murders he had helped to plan. He and several other men killed Rudolph Marfeo and Anthony Melei, who had defied Patriarca's order to shut down a gambling operation that had not been sanctioned. For his role in the double murder, he was sentenced to two life terms plus ten years. In 1985, the Rhode Island Supreme Court overturned his conviction because the essential prosecution witness who was involved with the murders and agreed to cooperate was suffering from Alzheimer's disease. The same government witness was also encouraged to lie by FBI agent Paul Rico in the trial of Maurice "Pro" Lerner, one of the seven involved in the murder. He then pled guilty to conspiracy, was credited for the two years he had already served and was released. In the past twenty years, he has been able to stay out of trouble and avoid prosecution.

During this time, George Lubell, a former corrections officer at Deer Island and Suffolk County House of Corrections at South Bay in Roxbury, was terminated for unnecessary force against inmates, according to records in 1994. Lubell was an associate of Gigi and believed to be a shooter in the crew. Lubell was known for his short fuse and propensity toward violence, along with his nasty disposition. During a drug buy in Bellingham Square, Chelsea, in 1995, he was shot in the face. The deal evidently went bad, but Lubell survived. He was also a suspect in the 1997 slaying of Charles Olivolo, a twenty-eight-year-old weight lifter and auto store clerk in Peabody. His decomposed body washed up in Boston Harbor. Lubell was also implicated in dealing drugs in South Bay County Jail. According to court documents, he and Suffolk County Sheriff L.T. Douglas Racca distributed Percocet, marijuana and anabolic steroids in the Boston area. Lubell was shot in the back outside of the Powerhouse Gym on Charger Street in Revere when he was shaking down a drug dealer. After the attack, Lubell went into the gym and requested that they call an ambulance. It appeared that the gunman fled on foot down Squire Road. He was described as a dark-haired male in his early twenties.

An unrelated investigation revealed further information on federal wiretaps from Town Line Ten Pin Bowling Alley. The wiretaps revealed the information about Lubell and Racca, Lubell's shooting and their drug ring.

A day after Gigi was shot at outside the Caravan Club, Jackie Salemme was in federal court answering an eight-count indictment that dated back to 1993, when he was operating a football-betting ring in Massachusetts and Rhode Island.

CHAPTER 7

THE TRIAL

In December 1996, Gigi, McConnell and Mele all took a trip out to Las Vegas first and then Arizona. During the trip, Gigi met with an undercover DEA agent who hammered out a deal to ship cocaine to him through the mail. The agent attempted to sell McConnell an automatic rifle for $10,000, but he declined. Gigi got to see his son and spend some time with him, and he needed to get away from all of the problems back home. On the day the men left for the trip, a federal grand jury had handed down an indictment of Gigi for a drug deal that took place in November that had been video and audio taped. Presumably, Smiley Mele had helped the government set up the surveillance.

It had been about two weeks since Gigi's attempted assassination, and things were looking up, or so it seemed. On December 14 at 7:30 a.m., as Gigi and McConnell were exiting the plane at Logan Airport on their return home from Arizona, they were greeted by U.S. Drug Enforcement agents, who arrested them as they stepped off the plane. Gigi asked the agents how they had known where he was. DEA special agent Anthony Roberto jokingly suggested that a tracking device had been implanted in his buttocks when he underwent surgery to remove the bullet from the shooting in Revere. Gigi was charged with possession of cocaine with intent to distribute and conspiracy to violate the narcotic laws. McConnell was charged with conspiracy. Two days later, on December 16, 1996, Gigi's brother Eddie was arrested in a separate case and charged with possession of cocaine and intent to distribute. Shortly after Gigi was put into custody, a warrant was served on his Nahant home. DEA agents searched the home and seized guns and bulletproof vests. U.S. District Court Magistrate Judge Robert Collings ruled that Gigi was a danger to the public and a possible flight risk, so he was ordered held without bail pending trial.

As Gigi was being held in jail without bail, the government was amping up its case against the New England mob. The U.S. federal district attorney was going to bill the alleged actions of the accused as a bloody struggle by a rogue faction attempting to take over the remnants of the New England mob. Assistant U.S. attorney Jeffrey Auerhahn was assigned to the case. He was going to put ten men on trial and place the majority of the blame on Robert "Bobby Russo" Carrozza. In his opening statements, Auerhahn stated, "This case will be about organized crime, the mafia, and about La Cosa Nostra." He went on to say, "The glue that holds it all together is that man—Bobby Russo." They planned to put Sean Cote and Mark Spisak on the stand to testify against their former friends. They were originally on the indictment but agreed to cooperate with the government. Defense lawyer Martin Weinberg countered in his opening by stating that the government's case was built on "professional criminals" and an FBI informant who were hoping to have their sentences reduced. The defendants included John Patti III, Eugene "Gino" Rida, Vincent "Gigi" Marino/Portalla, Nazzaro "Ralph" Scarpa, Paul DeCologero, Christopher Puopolo, Anthony Diaz and Robert "Bobby Russo" Carrozza. Three other men reached plea agreements prior to trial: Leo Boffoli, John Arciero and Enrico Ponzo.

The week before the trial was set to begin, Leo Boffoli entered into an agreement with the government. Assistant U.S. attorney Auerhahn asked that Boffoli be able to serve his time in protective custody and, upon release, enter into the Witness Protection Program. Boffoli was charged with conspiracy to murder, attempted murder, illegal use of a firearm and four counts of perjury. However, he ended up pleading guilty only to conspiracy to murder and one count of perjury. The government then requested a dismissal of the other charges.

Boffoli was one of 208 potential witnesses whom the government could have possibly called to testify. The coup de grâce of the government's evidence was the wiretap of the mafia induction ceremony held in Medford, Massachusetts, in October 1989.

The strangest moment of the trial occurred after Boston Police officer Ralph Amoroso was done testifying about the grisly scene of murder victim John Souza. When he stepped down from the witness stand, he walked past the members of the jury and shook hands with the defendant, Michael

The Final Days of the Boston Mob Wars

Romano Sr. Amoroso had walked a beat in East Boston for twelve years and Romano had spent his entire life there.

Just weeks before the government's star witness was due to testify, he died in custody. Sean Cote was dead at the age of twenty-seven. It appears that Cote died in his cell in the federal prison in Allenwood, Pennsylvania. His death was ruled a heart attack. Cote was in the Federal Witness Security Program waiting his turn to testify. It is believed that his long history of drug use and chain smoking led to his demise. His death did not have any indications of foul play. His death had a psychological effect on the prosecution for the moment, but that would soon pass.

The defense lawyers centered their arguments on the shootings of Michael Prochilo and Cirame and the stabbing of O'Toole. They used the fact that these men all could not identify their assailants and the witnesses all gave conflicting descriptions. One of the most damaging pieces of evidence was a letter dated December 16, 1996, written by Michael Romano and addressed to his cousin Gino Rida, who was incarcerated at the time. The letter suggests that Rida was having a problem with LaCorte and Romano was schooling him on how to handle the situation. The letter even referenced a club in Maverick Square, East Boston, that was unofficially owned by Carrozza and his half brother, J.R. Russo. In a P.S., Romano stated, "Raymond Jr. asks about you all the time. He knows how much I care about you." This loyalty to Patriarca on the part of Carrozza's followers might be surprising, since they helped engineer the end of his reign. The defense lawyers argued that the letter, while damaging, could not establish a causal relationship between these men and the crimes that they were on trial for. They went on to say that it was reasonable to believe that Romano might have possibly been bragging or blowing off steam, especially since the letter had overtones that Romano and Rida were possibly in danger and were name dropping out of fear, as a means of self-preservation.

During the three-month trial, the government paraded almost 120 witnesses and over three hundred evidence exhibits before the jury. The jury deliberated for almost two weeks. On January 12, 1999, the jury returned with a verdict. The jury found Anthony Ciampi guilty of illegal gambling. Paul DeCologero and Christopher Puopolo were acquitted of all charges, and the remaining defendants were acquitted on some of the charges. The jurors were unable to reach a verdict on fifty-three of those charges, the most serious ones, such as racketeering and murder. It appeared that the defense strategy of attacking the credibility of the government's five former mob witnesses, upon whom the prosecution relied heavily, had worked. Chief of the U.S. Attorney's Criminal Division James B. Farmer stated, "It's a case eminently worthy of retrial." First Assistant U.S. Attorney Mark Pearlstein said, "Fully expect to retry the charges on which the jury could not reach a verdict." Anthony Diaz chose to plead out early to the murder of Paul Strazzulla. According to the plea agreement, Diaz had to serve fifteen years.

Less than five months after the first trial, the government was already working on the preliminary hearings for the second trial. It was during one of these preliminary hearings that it was first brought to Judge Groton's attention that the DEA may have implanted a tracking device in the buttocks of Vincent Marino, aka Gigi Portalla. Apparently, the DEA agent had asked Gigi to sign a release form allowing them to remove the device. The agent admitted in court that the remarks were made but that he was only "joking." Attorney Sheketoff asked the court to order that the government come clean on the rumor of the tracking device. Later that day, U.S. attorney Donald Staern issued a statement saying, "We can confirm the U.S. Drug Enforcement Administration did not implant a tracking device in defendant Vincent M. 'Gigi Portalla' Marino's buttocks. We cannot speak, however, for any extraterrestrial beings. I hope this will finally put the matter behind us." Gigi informed Judge Groton in a statement at his arraignment saying, "They put an illegal device in my body. They did it during my surgery. There are no civil rights anymore. There's nothing left." Gigi's lawyer, Robert Sheketoff, addressed reporters later and stated, "The bottom line is if the government did this I'd be surprised if they admitted it. I'm not saying they did. The only way to really know is to open him up." Gigi had an X-ray taken of his buttocks, but it didn't show any device. Sheketoff asked the court to have an MRI done. It was denied on the grounds of cost and security. Gigi's family offered to pay the cost of the procedure and the added security costs, but still the request was denied.

Attorney Sheketoff informed the court that the only way to get to the bottom of this was to have Gigi undergo surgery. He went on to say that it was extremely unprofessional of the agent to make a comment like this, even if it was meant to be a joke, due to the fact that the technology is available for such a device. We may never know whether the device was implanted in him, since the courts refuse to allow surgery or an MRI.

Just days before the second trial was about to get underway, three of the defendants changed their pleas. Anthony Ciampi admitted to several murder attempts and the murder of Richard Devlin. Eugene Rida pled out to conspiracy to commit murder. The government dropped six other charges that would have sent him to prison for life. Nazzarro "Ralph" Scarpa pled guilty to four attempted murders. Ciampi received eighteen years according to his deal, while Scarpa and Rida each received ten years. The government also agreed to the dismissal of certain other charges in exchange for the guilty pleas.

An hour before opening statements were due to begin, Michael Romano Sr. entered into a plea agreement. According to the agreement, Romano pled guilty to conspiracy to commit murder in the aid of racketeering, interstate travel for unlawful activity and attempted assault. The murder charge was dismissed along with thirteen other counts. A twenty-one-year sentence was recommended for Romano. One month into the new trial, Robert "Bobby Russo" Carrozza took a plea agreement while he had already been in prison for almost ten years. The agreement only added two years to the sentence he was already serving. According to the agreement, he was exempt from testifying or cooperating with the government. He pled guilty to a felony charge of gambling across state lines.

Mob associate Darin Bufalino pled guilty to robbery and gun charges. The plea agreement stems from a bank robbery he committed with Sean Cote. He went into the Boston Five Branch at Northgate Shopping Plaza, jumped over the counter, brandished a weapon and grabbed $3,000 in cash. In 1984, Bufalino was charged with killing reputed Revere drug dealer Vincent DeNino, whose bullet-riddled body was found in the trunk of a car.

During the second trial, Gigi's girlfriend and Corrine, his mother, attended, as well as John Patti's wife. When the reporters asked them for a comment, Mrs. Portalla said, "He has a good heart. He loves God very much." While Gigi was in jail and going through the endless court proceedings of the first trial, his brother Louie passed away from a drug overdose. It seemed that

Mrs. Portalla couldn't help but stand by her son, fearing that she might lose another son to a long prison sentence.

In the closing arguments, the defense attempted once again to discredit the government witnesses. The main whipping boy was John "Smiley" Mele, a convicted drug dealer turned witness to save himself from a long prison term. They also attempted to discredit Jerry Matricia. A week later, the jury was done deliberating and returned guilty verdicts against both men. Gigi and Patti were both convicted on two RICO counts and conspiracy to murder in aid of racketeering. Gigi was sentenced to thirty-five years in prison on April 14, 2000.

Enrico Ponzo is still at large and is being sought by the Boston FBI office. He was arrested in 1994 for possession with intent to distribute cocaine and conspiracy to violate the narcotics laws. He failed to appear in court, and an arrest warrant was issued. In December 1994, the United States District Court issued another warrant charging him with unlawful flight from prosecution. In 1996, he was charged with aggravated assault in Everett, Massachusetts. On April 4, 1997, a federal grand jury indicted him for conspiracy to commit murder, interference with commerce by threats or violence, violent crimes in aid of racketeering, RICO violations and firearms violations. It is believed that he may be in Florida or Italy under an assumed name. The FBI is currently offering a $15,000 reward for his capture.

As a side note, before Rico Ponzo fled the coming indictments, he called Gigi's brother Eddie for a ride one night. Eddie picked him up, and while en route to their destination, a Saugus Police officer pulled them over. While the officer was checking Eddie's license and registration, Rico turned to Eddie and told him that if the cop wanted to arrest him, he was going to kill the cop. Eddie, reassuring Rico that murder wouldn't be necessary, was able to stay collected during this harrowing experience. The officer returned, proceeded to give Eddie a warning and allowed him and his passenger to go on their way. Eddie dropped Rico off and never saw him again. A few days later, some FBI agents stopped by to see Eddie. They asked if he had seen Rico or at least knew where he might be. Eddie denied all knowledge of Rico's whereabouts. The agents proceeded to tell him that had the officer who stopped them the other night attempted to take Rico into custody, Rico would have killed the cop and Eddie as well. Eddie quickly realized just how close he had come to being killed. This is just how uncertain life in the mob can be—one day you're friends with somebody and the next day he's your possible executioner.

CHAPTER 8

WHAT'S LEFT

In the decade that has followed since the mob war and the subsequent trials and convictions, much has changed in the New England mafia. No longer do you have the old-time street wise guys; today, they have a more corporate look about them. They still loan shark and run illegal bookmaking operations, but now it's on a much smaller scale. At the height of the mafia's power in the United States in the 1950s and 1960s, there were approximately five thousand members. Today, that number is much lower. However, the real strength of the mob was never in the number of made guys there were. The real strength was in the number of connected guys who take orders from the made guys. These guys number in the tens of thousands. There are always young Turks willing to do low-level crimes and work their way up the ladder to make a name for themselves. This new breed of wise guy is neither as smart nor as forward thinking as his predecessors. The old-time gangster grew up in a particular culture under specific economic conditions with limited educational and employment opportunities. The old-timers didn't come to this country with the intention of taking over the criminal world. They came here to work and build a better life, and circumstances altered the course for a few of them.

Today, the replacements choose to be wise guys. The traditional mob structure is crumbling. It can be compared to the end of the Roman Empire. The wolf is at the door, so to speak, and it's not the federal government. Instead, it's the Russians, Albanians, Chinese and other ethnic groups taking over. They are also much more brutal and fearless of the authorities and the consequences of their crimes; they view our worst prison as the Four Seasons when compared to the prisons in their homeland. In Providence, the Latin Kings and Asian gangs have become fully entrenched in the metropolitan area over the last fifteen years. They are newcomers and don't have the same national or international reach as the mob, but they are relentless in their pursuit to gain power and recognition. Patriarca member Guglielmeti was caught on a wiretap grumbling about the mob of today. He said, "So, now I mean it's like, ah, a whore in the neighborhood—you know, you stand here long enough, we'll use her."

Roughly during the same time that the Italian mob was at war with itself, a new and more violent Irish mob was on the rise in Charlestown. In 1992, George Sargent was brutally gunned down on a summer night outside a pizza parlor in Charlestown. He had provided information to police concerning criminal dealings in his neighborhood. The community left him lying in the street in a pool of his own blood and refused to cooperate with the police when questioned. In fact, no one even called the police. This was the code of silence that existed in Charlestown that had prevailed for decades. Between 1975 and 1992, the neighborhood had experienced forty-nine murders, thirty-three of which were never solved. The Irish mob was overrunning the small, heavily Irish community. These violent career criminals were preying on their own people. They had established a major PCP and cocaine distribution center. Because of the fierce ethnic tribalism that existed in this community, these criminals were able to operate with virtual impunity. When it became clear that Charlestown had a major drug problem, the DEA became involved. It joined forces with the Massachusetts State Police, the Boston Housing Police, the FBI, ATF and the U.S. Marshals.

After three long years of extensive investigations, they finally achieved tangible results. In order to find informants to help solve both the drug and murder cases, they arranged to protect witnesses who agreed to testify. The DEA even set up a hotline that allowed informants to stay completely anonymous. This went even further toward ending the tyranny that had held the residents hostage for so many years. In July 1994, forty defendants were indicted on charges including racketeering, murder, conspiracy, drug trafficking and armed robbery. One indictment charged that two of the defendants paid hired killers $5,000 to murder anyone who tried to encroach on their territory.

The Final Days of the Boston Mob Wars

Today, the Irish mob has been replaced in Charlestown with yuppies and white-collar professionals looking to raise their families in historic quaint three-deckers with backyards the size of postage stamps. The DEA was effective in shutting down the Irish mob for good in Charlestown. It hasn't been that effective with the Italian mob. Angiulo said it best: "Crime doesn't pay unless it's organized."

The other attack that the mafia has had to deal with is the affliction of drugs. Cocaine and heroin have made the mob a ton of money; however, they have hurt more than they have helped. Drug trafficking has spread chaos among the mob hierarchy and forced the mafia into Chapter Eleven. The old-timers never touched drugs; they didn't deal them and they especially didn't use them or tolerate anyone who did. From 1989 to 1995, the last mob war was riddled with heavy drug use by several of its members. Had these men not been involved with narcotics during this time frame, the rogue faction may have been more successful, the death toll may have been much lower and the end result would have been drastically different.

The other mitigating factors that have added to the mob's demise can be contributed to the neighborhoods that were once considered mob strongholds. Neighborhoods that were once unique for ethnic tribalism, fierce parochialism and partisan politics have changed.

When Jerry Angiulo was sentenced in 1986, the North End of Boston was almost 100 percent Italian-American; today, it is less than 40 percent. This exodus of people in the old neighborhoods left a vacuum that was filled by immigrants of other nationalities. Another factor is that the Generation X gangsters don't adhere to the old rules. They scoff at the old rules, shoot at their elders and grab the drug money as quick as it comes in. Years ago, these guys kept their mouths shut and served their time without complaint. Today, it doesn't matter whether a guy is facing one month or one thousand years; the first thought is, *can I give up some information to save myself?*

The original infrastructure of the American mafia that was established by Lucky Luciano was set up to insulate the bosses. The rules were made to establish order. Today, there is anarchy. The new generation has taken traditional mob values like loyalty, honor and family and bastardized them to their criminal ends. Loyalty has turned into betrayal. The FBI has been singing the death song of the American mob for quite some time, but it hasn't yet been able to kill it. The mob's ability to survive stems from its ability to reinvent itself. The average gangster is lost in a complex world of moral relativism, and like his postmodern contemporaries, he is overwhelmed and confused. Day after day, lines are blurring into one another. Roles are shifting, things are changing. Even in the mob, nobody knows what's what. The reality is that chaos reigns when rules should bring order. This brings to light the foolishness of a life in organized crime without the organization. This is the end result when you break the vows of the criminal covenant. Loyalty to an organization and its boss is what makes organized crime work. However, a loyalty rooted in fear will eventually collapse.

What the FBI and the government don't seem to understand is that there will always be someone to fill the place of the mobsters who are sent to prison. For some people, the routine of a normal life—that is, work, paying bills and living an honest life—is seen as the curse of the stupid and weak. These men are under the belief that money and pleasure bring happiness and contentment. They ignore the extreme guilt, paranoia and greed that gradually rip their lives apart.

On a cold January morning in 2005, David Achille, son of a capo in the Patriarca family, headed to a construction site in India Point Park, Providence, to settle a dispute over union job assignments. The Rhode Island State Police allege that David's father, Joseph Achille, received the order from top-level mobsters to shoot two laborers in the kneecaps. While the mob was getting ready to flex its muscle on the waterfront, state police were monitoring telephone calls. They were tipped off to a potential confrontation. They moved in and arrested David Achille and a union laborer. In Achille's car was a loaded handgun. Rhode Island State Police detectives say that they thwarted a potentially bloody confrontation at the job site. The father-and-son duo ended up pleading guilty to a variety of felony charges stemming from the aborted shooting; they are each currently serving a one-year sentence.

In 2008, federal prosecutors brought to light a remade New England mob, headed by Arthur Gianelli, a bookmaker, loan shark and money launderer who looks more like Gordon Gekko in *Wall Street*. The FBI refers to the Gianelli crew or gang as the Gianelli Group. Gianelli is the brother-in-law of ex–federal agent John Connolly. It appears that

The Final Days of the Boston Mob Wars

Gianelli's men opted for betting slips rather than computers. They control illegal gaming machines, football cards, offshore betting in Costa Rica and other racketeering enterprises. During his trial, it came out that Boston Bruin Hall of Famer Gerry Cheevers took a loan from Gianelli that was brokered through Phil Castinetti, who is from Revere and owns Sportsworld, the largest sports memorabilia store in New England. The interest rate on Cheevers's loan was 150 percent. It seems that Cheevers defaulted on the loan and Gianelli dispatched mob enforcer Phil Puopolo to Castinetti to ensure that Cheevers paid. According to the prosecution, Gianelli committed hundreds of crimes that netted him millions of dollars. This made it harder for him to launder.

All loan sharking took place with the blessing of New England underboss Carmen "Cheeseman" DiNunzio, who lives in East Boston and spends his days working in the North End at his cheese shop, Fresh Cheese. There, he meets with people, and on occasion he also meets with Manocchio at a restaurant in the suburbs. In 1992, he and his brother Anthony, along with nine other men, were indicted for racketeering and extortion. They attempted to take over an Indian gaming hall. A year later, he pled guilty to the extortion count, which included shaking down a Las Vegas gambler for $27,000. He was sentenced to four years in prison.

The Federal Bureau of Investigations in Boston has seemed to abandon all ethical pretense. From the handling of Joseph "the Animal" Barboza to the mess created by the Whitey Bulger case, there has been an erosion of trust that has weakened the faith of the American people in its top law enforcement agency. Indeed, an alarming number of cultural problems has exploded in our country since 1960, and it appears that the FBI has been plagued by them as well. Our standards of morality expressed in our laws and customs have been relaxed, abandoned or judicially overruled. The FBI has been besieged by scandal concerning its methods of crime fighting in recent years. The devil's deal that agent Connolly entered into with Bulger and Flemmi is questionable, at best. The ethical and constitutional questions that these cases raise are alarming. Then, a federal judge orders the DEA to inform Gigi as to whether a tracking device was implanted in him, and we are to take their word on the matter. In June 1999, when the *New York Times* asked the FBI if it had ever used such a tracking device, interestingly, Paul Bresson, bureau spokesman, stated, "This is going to fall into the no comment department."

We rationalize and justify abhorrent behavior under the umbrella that these men are criminals and therefore the end justifies the means. That mentality will have every citizen in this country handing over his or her civil liberties for law and order. These cases give us a glimpse into the character and quality of our top law enforcement agencies' and agents' morality. Uninhibited by the restraints of public appearance, the agents are able to obtain a practiced level of deceit. Without reasonable and responsible limits on law enforcement agencies, their actions will destroy individual lives and, eventually, the fabric of civilized society. Conventional wisdom dictates that morality cannot be legislated or indoctrinated through policy. The complex question that arises then is whether a common standard of morality is even possible, and if it is, how important is it to the fabric of our society? Discussing this controversial issue is like marching through a minefield of objection. The FBI's decision to cover up the scandals seems to be plausibly logical, considering its stake in the matter. To single out agents like John Connolly as villains is to ignore the extraordinarily powerful culture and political forces that have long dominated the FBI. Their often illegal actions are an abuse of power and border on obstruction of justice. This seemingly unprecedented behavior is especially bothersome. Scorn and ridicule are the backlash of years of secret deals. Although it may seem like an elusive ideal to instill some outside monitoring of these agencies and their policies concerning the handling of informants, a moral compass must be established. Despite outside pressure and political limitations, the inescapable conclusion is that the FBI will be stigmatized and have its informants' information undermined for some time, despite a professed willingness to succumb to closer monitoring and a change in policies. These are not grand expectations or elusive ideals, but rather an imperfect system attempting to adjust for the greater good.

The FBI's government misconduct mainly centers on mob snitch Whitey Bulger, who has been an informant since 1970. Another informant was Robert "Bobby" Donati, a driver for Capo Vincent "the Animal" Ferrara, who was found stabbed to death in his white Cadillac in 1991. The next disturbing deal concerned Anthony "the Saint" St. Laurant, a made member of the Patriarca family. He pled guilty to gambling charges and received only a ten-month sentence. We can only speculate as to the information that he gave the FBI for an easy sentence like that. His co-conspirator, Robert "Bobby" Deluca, received five years. Obviously, he wasn't working with the government. Angelo "Sonny" Mercurio was believed to have helped the FBI bug the mafia induction ceremony. His alleged informant status was kept secret from a federal judge. This was also one of the biggest FBI surveillance coups in history. Besides Connolly, there were alleged questionable actions carried out by agent Paul Rico and Dennis Condon, not to mention how many retired or deceased agents were involved in the coverup of the Deegan case.

In 2001, a U.S. House Investigating Committee began holding hearings looking into the misconduct of the Boston FBI office. The hearings were interrupted by the terrorist attacks on 9-11. Former FBI agent Dennis Condon, who had heard that the hearings would be reconvening, stated, "Don't you have anything better to do?" The House Government Reform Committee has been listening to evidence stating that for decades Boston FBI agents provided tips to organized crime leaders to help them eliminate witnesses against them, sent innocent men to prison for life, lied to other law enforcement agencies and covered up crimes committed by their informants. The major goal of the committee is to identify how much FBI headquarters knew about the Boston office's misconduct. Massachusetts representative Bill Delahunt, who presides on the committee, stated, "What we have revealed here is an institution in dire need of reform, with no accountability, no transparency and a total lack of controls."

Now the families of two women—the widow of a small-time mobster who has been missing for years and the widow of a Tulsa multimillionaire who was killed gangland style at his country club—whose bodies were found in a shallow grave along the outer reaches of Boston Harbor are suing the FBI. The two women whose bodies were found were girlfriends of Stephen Flemmi. Their bodies were only discovered after another Bulger associate led police to the burial grounds. These lawsuits have put the Justice Department in a difficult situation. To date, there have been six lawsuits filed and more are expected. The problem is that the burden of proof is lower than in the criminal trial, in which agent Connolly was acquitted of the most serious charges, including complicity to murder. Also, there may be further damaging revelations. Some of the damaging evidence that has been introduced was hidden in FBI files. The information stated that Vincent Flemmi, who murdered Teddy Deegan in 1965, was an informer for the FBI. Despite knowing this, the FBI allowed another of its informants to testify that four innocent men had committed the killing. Then there was the 1965 memo to J. Edgar Hoover saying that Flemmi had committed the killing and would kill again but that "the informant's potential outweighs the risks." Attorney Libby has found the government's answer to his lawsuit paradoxical.

He represents the estate of Roger Wheeler, the chairman of Telex, who was killed in 1981 on orders from Bulger. Attorney Libby was notified the same day that Mr. Connolly was convicted. The Justice Department stated that it was moving to dismiss his lawsuit on the grounds that the statute of limitations had expired. Libby stated, "There is some irony in the government saying the Wheeler family should have known, from a half continent away, twenty years ago, that government agents were committing murder."

Charles Pouty was sent to the Boston FBI field office in 1997 as part of a team of FBI and Justice Department investigators sent there to investigate allegations of misconduct. These allegations were brought to light at a hearing being presided over by United States district judge Mark L. Wolf. Pouty and the team quickly and hastily produced a report that found no wrongdoing within the five-year statute of limitations. A year later, at another hearing with Judge Wolf, even more evidence came to light, most of which was cited as misconduct at Connolly's trial. One of the acts that the team missed occurred in December 1994, when agent Connolly tipped off Bulger about the coming indictments, which gave him ample time to flee. Some officials have been critical of Pouty and his team. However, in their defense, the team only had five weeks to look into twenty-five years' worth of questionable activity. When reviewing the evidence that has been brought to light against the Boston FBI field office, it becomes apparent that there is a culture of concealment within the FBI. The bureau would get itself into a protective mentality where it cared less about justice and more about protecting itself from agent mistakes.

In the end, Connolly was sentenced to forty years in prison for his part in the murder of a Miami gambling executive in 1982. Miami-Dade circuit judge Stanford Blake rejected the defense's claims that a four-year statute of limitations had expired on Connolly's second-degree murder conviction in the killing of John Callahan. Judge Blake stated that the motion on that issue was filed past a ten-day deadline but was probably legally correct. There almost certainly will be an appeal on this case. It is doubtful if it will be overturned.

Gigi's life is disturbing in a productive way. He takes center stage in this Shakespearean tragicomedy. He is a paradox of greatness and wretchedness. Gigi is no bumbling simpleton. He is thoughtful, polite, reflective and extremely compassionate. Yet his father's past actions have had powerful consequences that have reverberated into his life. Big Eddie Marino inevitably bequeathed his traits to his sons, Eddie and Gigi.

In recent years, Eddie Portalla has had legal troubles of his own. On Friday, May 20, 2005, he was found guilty in a federal court on charges of cocaine distribution conspiracy and money laundering. In January 2003, an undercover DEA agent posed as a drug dealer who knew Jason and Salvatore Carrillo. The undercover agent met with Eddie Portalla at his business, Wakefield Communications, on Western Avenue in Lynn, Massachusetts. During the two meetings with the undercover agent, he informed Portalla that he was a drug dealer and that he had cash from illegal sales of drugs. Eddie sold the agent cellphones and activated them under fictitious names at both meetings. The DEA had wiretaps of Portalla saying that they could turn a telephone on under any name or they could buy a track telephone and put it under a fake name. The track telephones can also be bought in a store and turned on under a false name from home. Weeks prior to the meetings with the undercover agent, another man came into the store and asked Eddie if he could launder some money for him. Eddie told him no and then called the FBI to report the incident. The telephone call was never mentioned by the prosecution. The sales of the telephones were charged as two counts of money laundering. The government also presented evidence that Eddie provided the Carrillos with false W-2 forms. These forms stated that they were employed at his business as sales associates earning between $70,000 and $80,000 a year. It was the government's assertion that these W-2 forms helped the Carrillos obtain a two-bedroom oceanfront condominium, two luxury apartments and various high-end automobiles.

During the eight-day trial, the government was able to establish that Eddie knew that the Carrillos were selling cocaine and that he sold them phones knowing that they would be used to violate the narcotic laws. Eddie was originally offered a plea agreement that stated he would have to serve two years. He refused the plea on the basis that he didn't feel as though he had committed a crime. He never touched any drugs, he was never present during any of the drug deals and he came in on the investigation only during the last two weeks. He didn't care where the money came from, he just wanted to sell telephones and make money. As for the W-2 forms, the Carrillos had a thriving business: they owned Miss Q Billiards in Malden. However, they couldn't show enough income to qualify for a mortgage. Therefore, they asked a friend to say that they worked for him so they could get a mortgage, and he did them a favor. The government had a mortgage broker on a wiretap informing them how to launder money so they could provide a down payment and cash assets. The funny thing is that the government never pressed charges against the mortgage broker. Eddie was sentenced to ten years. Currently, he has been able to overturn the sentence and is due to be released. He denies any involvement in the drug conspiracy and feels that he is a victim of his last name.

In recent years, the mob has used the federal prison system as a way of networking and increasing its criminal connections. Going to prison has always been an occupational hazard for mob guys. The constant police scrutiny, wiretaps and surveillance eventually lead to criminal cases, which lead to prison sentences.

Anthony W. Fiore Jr. and Richard Gomes are both Patriarca associates and were placed center stage during John Gotti Jr.'s trial. Prosecutors attempted to undermine Gotti's claim that he had retired from the Gambino family. The prosecution introduced evidence that Gotti was treated as a mafia boss while incarcerated. The evidence was a photograph of Fiore and Gotti posing in the prison yard. Fiore has been in prison for the past fifteen years for running an armored car robbery gang. Another piece of evidence the prosecution introduced was a recorded prison conversation in which Gotti instructed his lawyer to send $500 to Gomes in prison. Gomes was a close personal friend of John Gotti Sr., the most famous mob boss in America. John Gotti Jr. stated on tape, "He was very dear to my father. I know he's in jail, I know he's, that he's broke, people came through here and told me this. This is a great guy. This is a real man." Gomes had served nearly twenty years for shooting two men outside a wiener shop in Olneyville. He died at the age of seventy-three, shortly after being released from prison. On the wall of his apartment in Providence hung photos of his friends, Gotti and Patriarca Sr. Rhode Island State Police major O'Donell said, "Fiore has to have power to be in Gotti's presence. It helps Fiore gain power and prestige." Fiore is also a lifelong friend of mob hit man Tillinghast.

Carrozza was released from prison on March 24, 2008, at the age of sixty-eighty. His present status is unknown. J.R. Russo lost his bout with leukemia in June 1998 at Springfield Federal Prison Hospital. Deluca was released in June 2004 and has been keeping a low profile since his release. The Massachusetts and Rhode Island State Police task forces are keeping a close watch on these men as they are being released from prison. Law enforcement realizes just how unstable the peace of the underworld really is and is vigilantly watching to ensure that another war doesn't break out.

Many law enforcement officials have claimed that the mafia of today is nothing but a bunch of thugs running around appropriating the title "mafia" to give themselves an inflated sense of importance. Former president Lyndon Johnson's Commission on Law Enforcement and the Administration of Justice stated in its report that there was a nationwide criminal entity consisting of thousands of criminals "working within structures as complex as those of any large corporation, subject to laws more rigidly enforced than those of legitimate government." It all began with Lucky Luciano's evolutionary adaptation of the Sicilian mob. He welcomed doing business with outside ethnic groups and established treaties with these groups in order to allow both groups to benefit and prosper. He realized that without efficiency and profits, no group would be able to survive for very long. The changes he implemented are perhaps his greatest contribution to the continuing longevity of organized crime.

The mob will undoubtedly keep its stranglehold on the northeastern part of the United States because there is a large contingent of Italian-Americans living in the area. It is important to remember that the remorseless, deviant sociopaths defame the very ethnic banner of Italian-American that they carry so proudly. The trouble with America today is that there are absolutely no obligations attached to living here. We've broken out of our social shackles and are free to follow our own bliss. Not to mention the economic classes within the organization.

Perhaps the best secret to the success of organized crime has been the American public's fascination with these men of honor. From the days of George Raft and James Cagney to *The Sopranos*, the public has been cheering for the wise guy. It is important to remember that this country was founded by men who broke the law to escape British rule. This may be why we raise these men to iconic status. Although we are tempted to glorify these men and their lifestyle, we need to see them as they are. These men are broken; their lives are void of meaning because they worship at the altar of the almighty dollar. They wake up every morning and perform their daily tasks, all the while searching for something they will never find: peace and contentment.

Nobody in the mob today wants to be a boss or in any position of power. This is because the title becomes a bull's-eye for the FBI. They also have to keep a watchful eye out for guys who are looking to sell them out. These guys are smart, clever and fun to be around. You could go out to eat and have a few drinks with them and you'll laugh all night long. The time you spend with them can also be potentially dangerous. Theirs is a dangerous world best observed from a safe distance.

Gigi's life is a parable about life and crime. Most of the guys he hung around with are dead, in prison, moved out of the neighborhood or are keeping a low profile. Still, in retrospect, he fared better than most when you consider that many kids he grew up with died tragically by Revere mainstays—drugs and a bullet.

As the seventeenth-century French philosopher François duc de la Rochefoucauld said, "It is more shameful to distrust one's friends than to be deceived by them." This quote seems to sum up life in the mafia.

BIBLIOGRAPHY

NEWSPAPERS

Boston American, September 16, 1960.
———, September 24, 1960.
Boston Globe, April 7, 1987.
———, January 16, 1999.
———, October 2, 1998.
Boston Herald, February 21, 1997.
———, March 27, 2000.
———, May 27, 1999.
———, September 30, 1999.
Chelsea Record, November 26, 1996.
Lynn Daily Evening Item, May 25, 1999.
Worcester Telegram and Gazette, January 13, 1999.
———, March 3, 2000.
———, October 14, 1998.

OTHER SOURCES

Boston Magazine, 1997.
FBI field reports
Maloney, J.J. "The Great Brinks Robbery." *Crime Magazine*.
U.S. Attorney's Office transcript of conversation, October 29, 1989.

ABOUT THE AUTHOR

William J. Craig resides in Revere, Massachusetts, with his wife and four children. He has served honorably in the United States Army and Air Force. He is a graduate of Gordon College in Wenham. He has previously written books on Fort Devens and Revere.